MILESTONES
IN THE
LIFE OF THE JEW

MILESTONES
IN THE
LIFE OF THE JEW

A BASIC GUIDE TO BELIEF AND RITUAL

by Donald G. Frieman

BLOCH PUBLISHING COMPANY

NEW YORK

0R2/84

CONTENTS

"One loves God only by dint of knowledge, and the degree of love corresponds to the degree of knowledge."
  Maimonides (Yad Chazakah, Hilchos Teshuvah 10.6)

This book has been written for the many men and women who truly desire to understand the background, history and abiding concepts found in the way Jews observe the rites marking the milestones in their lives. For the first time in one volume, the traditional point of view has been set forth and explained in terms readily comprehensible to the layman.

The guiding principle for this volume has been to set down the basic laws and traditions surrounding each of these milestones. I have found, all too often, that individuals possess only a fragmentized knowledge of these rites and lack a genuine understanding of its foundations. As these concepts are brought into proper focus, the rich heritage of the Jewish people will become readily apparent.

I am greatly indebted to many people, Rabbis and laymen, who have encouraged me to write this book. I particularly recall a group of enthusiastic women from Temple B'nai Sholom of Rockville Centre, N.Y. who listened to my series of lectures and encouraged me in this endeavor. I am indebted to Rabbi Reuben Katz, Rabbi David Moseson and Rabbi Isaac Freeman, who most carefully read the manuscript and offered many helpful comments. Most especially, I wish to express my appreciation to Rabbi Harry Halpern, my guide and mentor in life, for his helpful comments and encouragement. Invaluable aid in editing the text was provided by my brother, Alan, as well as Mrs. Samuel Alexander and Mrs. Morton Leifman. My appreciation also to my secretary, Mrs. Jerry Gellis, who devoted long hours in typing the manuscript. Acharon, acharon chaviv to my beloved helpmate, Rhoda, who particularly devoted hours without end to this work and provided the encouragement to see this work completed.

It should be noted that the transliteration of the Hebrew words has been made in accordance with the Ashkenazic pronunciation of Hebrew.

I wish to express my appreciation to the Jewish Publication Society of America for their kind permission to quote from their 1917 translation of the Holy Scriptures.

It is my fond hope that this book will add to an understanding and love of our great Jewish heritage.

Donald G. Frieman

January 1965

CHAPTER ONE

INTRODUCTION TO JEWISH LAW

According to Jewish law, may a newborn son be named after a beloved aunt? How long after a baby's birth is the *Bris* to be held? May weddings be performed between Passover and Shavuos? How long is the period of mourning known as *Shivah?*

These are some of the questions frequently asked concerning the great milestones of life as observed by Jews. To understand the observances of the Jewish tradition, one must be able to distinguish between a basic law and a peripheral custom. Often one finds a local custom zealously observed, while a basic law is overlooked. The individual must, therefore, begin a study of Jewish rites, rituals and customs with an analysis of the sources of Jewish law.

One need not be a lawyer to understand some fundamental concepts of American law and custom and to be able to evaluate their importance. According to American custom, it is proper for a man to remove his hat when entering an elevator of an apartment house, but certainly all of us realize that he would not receive a court summons for failing to do so. We also recognize that if a person overstayed his time at a parking meter, he would be subject to a fine of a few dollars. Increasingly severe penalties would be incurred for robbery and murder.

In the same manner, one must study Jewish law to learn what is basic and important on the one hand, and what may be nothing more than a local tradition on the other. This understanding of the sources of Jewish practice will place the law, custom and tradition associated with the milestones in the life of the Jew into proper perspective, leading to an appreciation of these rituals as expressions of the Jewish tradition.

SOURCES OF JEWISH LAW
THE TORAH

The Torah consists of the five books of the Bible—Genesis, Exodus, Leviticus, Numbers, and Deuteronomy. Just as the Holy Ark, containing the Torah, is the focal point to which the synagogue is oriented, so the Torah is the central guide for Jewish law. In view of the Divine inspiration of the Torah, Jews consider it eternal, i.e., its principles are as fresh and valid today as they were hundreds of years ago. Reverence for and acceptance of the Torah are the foundation of Jewish law and its interpretation.

It must be realized that not all of Jewish law can be found in the Torah, although the Torah does contain those guiding principles from which Jewish law and its interpretation spring. A parallel may be found by comparing the Torah to the Constitution of the United States. Although the Constitution is a brief document of only seven or eight pages, the shelves of law libraries are filled with thousands of volumes based on the Constitution—establishing additional laws in its spirit and enforcing the ideas and ideals set forth in that document.

Similarly, Jews look to the Torah as authoritative on all basic traditions and consider the laws set forth *Me'deoraisah* (in the Torah) as particularly binding. They seek to understand every word in the Torah as their guide in life. It is, therefore, important to our comprehension of the milestones of life to cite the Biblical references from which the Rabbis interpreted the law.

THE TALMUD

Once the Jewish people accepted the Torah, containing the history, the moral and ethical teachings, as well as the basic laws for religious practice as their authority, there arose a group who began to teach and to explain the Torah to the people. Gradually, their explanations of the law were organized into what we know today as the *Mishnah.* The *Mishnah,* which is part of the *Talmud,* sought to explain the laws as set forth in the Torah. Rabbi Judah HaNasi was the great compiler of the oral tradition of the *Mishnah,* which was completed around the year 250 of the Common Era. This compilation became the authoritative interpretation of the Torah.

No sooner was the *Mishnah* completed, than the Rabbis realized that it could neither encompass all the situations in one's life, nor cover new situations which were constantly developing. But since, in each situation, the Rabbis were always called upon to give rulings about proper conduct—conduct in accordance with the *Mitzvos* (religious ordinances) of the Torah, they continued to expand their explanations and add new ones. They felt that the *Mishnah,* although originally thought to be complete, needed further development. From numerous experiences, from cases presented to the Rabbis and from questions asked of the Rabbis, the *Gemorah,* which sought to expand the explanations of the *Mishnah,* was written. The *Gemorah* was completed around the year 500 of the Common Era. The *Mishnah* and the *Gemorah* together comprise the *Talmud,* a compendium of the great debates held by the Rabbis on Jewish law, as well as a record of their decisions. In addition, the *Talmud* contains a wealth of Jewish lore, sayings and stories which illustrated the topics under discussion.

THE CODES

The *Talmud* served as a very full and complete explanation of Jewish traditions and rituals. However, it was found that the "sea of the *Talmud*" was so vast that it was somewhat difficult to locate all the specific references on any one subject, since they were spread throughout this immense work. The Rabbis then began to codify the laws and set them in order, according to subject matter, so that one would be able to find them more easily. One of the most famous of these codes was written by Rabbi Moses ben Maimon, better known as Maimonides (1135–1204). Finding that the *Talmud* was no longer studied by the average Jew and that a new handbook of Jewish law was needed, he wrote the book *Mishne Torah,* in which he sought to arrange, in a methodical and logical manner, the laws set forth in the *Talmud.* The *Mishne Torah* is still studied today.

Other people also began to codify Jewish law. Rabbi Asher ben Jechiel (1250–1320), who became the spiritual leader in the community of Toledo in Spain, made an abstract of the material contained in the *Talmud,* as it was interpreted and supplemented by other authorities. His son, Rabbi Jacob ben Asher, wrote another code, in the same methodical manner as did Maimonides, and called his code *Arba Turim.*

The most popular and respected code of Jewish law was

written by Rabbi Joseph Caro, called the *Shulchan Aruch* (The Prepared Table). He felt that he had "prepared the feast," and that anyone could now "help himself" in order to understand the law. The *Shulchan Aruch* seeks to deal, as did the *Talmud*, with Jewish law and practice wherever the Jew might be: in the home, in the synagogue or at business. The *Shulchan Aruch* was published for the first time in the year 1567, was well received by the Jewish community and ultimately became the standard of Jewish law and observance. Rabbis in later years commented on the *Shulchan Aruch* and further elucidated the laws and customs which were set forth by Rabbi Joseph Caro in his work. Today, the *Shulchan Aruch* still serves as one of the basic keys to Jewish law and tradition.

RESPONSA

From the sixteenth century on, the major method of interpreting Jewish law became the *Responsa*. As the word indicates, *responsa* are answers to questions asked of Rabbis. Individuals would ask a Rabbi a question on a current problem; the Rabbi would give his *responsum* (answer), basing his reason on supporting statements in the Bible, the *Talmud* or the *Shulchan Aruch*. In this way, Jewish law found itself in continual development, seeking answers to the problems and questions of each new generation and time. This is the procedure presently used in interpreting and expanding Jewish law.

OTHER SOURCES OF TRADITION

Understanding the milestones in the life of the Jew requires this basic comprehension of the structure and development of Jewish practice. Apart from this, one must bear in mind that many practices have arisen outside of this legal framework. Those are the practices of custom —not law. While many of these customs are meaningful and are a complement to the law, others are contrary to it. Clearly, one would wish to encourage the former while abolishing the latter. Some illustrations will be helpful.

The *Bar Mitzvah* is a comparatively new ceremony in Jewish life. One can find no laws for *Bar Mitzvah* in the Torah, the *Talmud* or the *Shulchan Aruch*, yet it has been a great force in increasing the amount of Jewish education received by boys in our own day. The spiritual experience of the *Bar Mitzvah* boy brings him closer to his faith and to his people. In this day of equality for women, where the home is no longer the central source of Jewish education for the girl, the encouragement of the *Bas Mitzvah*, a twentieth-century addition to Jewish practice, has led to a religious education for girls. As such, it should not only be retained, but its practice ought to be expanded.

On the other hand, it seems customary today to bring cake and liquor to the cemetery at the time of the unveiling and dedication of the tombstone. The practice of this custom is widespread, and many Jews regard it as a law.

Jewish law, however, prohibits this practice and regards it as a desecration of the cemetery.

The milestones in the life of the Jew have been embellished with many local rituals stemming particularly from various east European communities as well as from sections of the United States. When analyzing the highlights of birth, *Bar Mitzvah,* marriage and death in the life of the Jew, we shall differentiate between law, custom, rite, folklore and superstition which have, at times, beclouded Jewish practices. Jews have a living, vibrant, meaningful faith which will become increasingly apparent through this systematic study of the milestones.

CHAPTER TWO

BIRTH—*BRIS*—NAMING THE CHILD

BIRTH

The miracle of birth is certainly a blessing from the Almighty. In spite of this, few references to Jewish concepts of birth may be found either in the Bible or in later sources.

The Bible does contain one specific reference to a woman's conduct during pregnancy: a warning (in the Book of Judges) is given to Samson's mother, who is told not to drink wine while she is with child, lest doing so influence the character of her unborn son. This reference indicates that the ancients believed that the mother's diet during gestation influenced not only the health, but also the personality of her offspring.

The *Talmud* teaches that each life is precious. The unborn child in its mother's womb, however, is not yet considered a living creature. This fact becomes particularly important, of course, when a crisis occurs during pregnancy or childbirth necessitating a decision as to whether the life of the mother or the embryo ought to be saved. According to Jewish law, the mother's life is saved at the expense of the embryo. Once the greatest part of the child has proceeded forth from the womb, however, it is considered a living creature, and the life of the newborn may not be ignored in safeguarding the life of the mother.

NAMING THE CHILD

There are no Jewish laws concerning the naming of the child. Much of what Jews observe today in this area is custom, folklore or superstition.

Ashkenazic Jews frequently memorialize a deceased relative by bestowing his name upon a newborn child. However, they do not use the names of a living relative, because of their belief that a person's name carries with it both the power and the characteristics of that person. Naming a child for a living relative would, therefore, they believe, reduce the power and shorten the life of that relative. Similarly, the name of a relative who died early in life would not be selected, lest a similar fate await the newborn. This appears to be a custom of Teutonic origin and is found only among the Ashkenazim. The Sephardim do not observe it.

Those who read the Bible find that children were never named after relatives, either those who were living or those who had passed on. None of the twenty-one kings of Judah, for example, were named after a predecessor, or even after the great King David, who was the founder of a large family.

In Biblical days, each individual had a single name, such as Abraham, Solomon or David. Two names were not needed to identify anyone. Later on, when the need arose, a person became known by his father's name in addition to his own name. This is how a man or woman is identified in the synagogue today. One uses the first name, then the word *ben* (the son of) and then the father's first name. For example, a man named *Yitzchak*, whose father's name was *Levi*, would be called *Yitzchak ben Levi*. For women, the first name is followed by the word *bas* (the daughter of) and then the name of her father.

The custom of using names of deceased relatives only was unknown in Talmudic days. The *Talmud* tells us, for example, of two Rabbis, grandfather and grandson, both named Gamaliel. Gamaliel II was born while Gamaliel I was still alive. The only objection seemed to be to the confusion which might result from the duplication of names.

Most parents today bestow upon their offspring a pleasant-sounding English name and then select a distinctly separate Hebrew name, usually memorializing the name of a deceased relative. This has not always been the practice. In the days of the Bible, the names selected would have special significance. An illustration may be found in the Book of Genesis, in the beautiful story of Abraham and his childless wife Sarah. Although advanced in years, she greatly desired to have a child. Three angels in the form of men appeared and were hospitably received by Abraham. Before the angels left, they told Abraham that in the course of time, he was to have a son. Upon hearing this, Sarah was so overjoyed that she laughed. When the child was born, they named him *Yitzchak,* which is the Hebrew word for "laughter."

Because the ancients believed that a name carried with it certain magical significance, parents named their children only after serious contemplation of the meaning of the name. They wished it to describe either characteristics already evident in him or attributes they hoped he would attain. A boy born with particularly fair skin might be named *Laban,* meaning "white." At times, children were named after animals. The name *Jonah,* for example, means "dove"; *Deborah* means "bee." Some parents wished to have their children's name bear a part of God's name and used it either as a prefix or a suffix, as in the names *JO*shua and Ezeki*EL.* Although the number of names that may be bestowed upon newborn children is endless, it is significant that Jews throughout the ages have attempted to name their children with Hebrew names relating to the Bible, to God or to the Jewish people.

A boy is given his name during the ceremony of the *Bris*. A girl is named in the synagogue when the father is called to the Torah for an *Aliyah*, generally on the Sabbath following her birth (although she may be named whenever the Torah is read).

It is interesting to note that in early times it was the custom to name the child immediately upon birth. Later, the naming became postponed because it was feared that the name presented a "handle" with which the baby could be reached by the angel of death. It was thought that if the naming were postponed for several days, the angel of death would not be able to reach the child during the precarious first few days of life.

SHALOM ZACHAR

Throughout the ages in every land the Jews have been persecuted and have had very few occasions to celebrate. Therefore, they rejoiced whenever it was possible. One such occasion was the *Shalom Zachar* (welcome to the son), which was celebrated on the Friday evening prior to the *Bris*. This was an additional time for feasting and an opportunity for study. As neighbors and friends gathered in the home of the newborn, the Rabbi delivered a special lecture in honor of the occasion and offered his blessing to the child. The *Shalom Zachar,* although a beautiful custom which should be encouraged, is not generally observed in many localities.

BRIS

This is My covenant, which ye shall keep, between Me and you and thy seed after thee: every male among you shall be circumcised. And ye shall be circumcised in the flesh of your foreskin; and it shall be a token of the covenant betwixt Me and you. And he that is eight days old shall be circumcised among you, every male throughout your generations . . . (Genesis 17:10–12)

The Rabbis always referred to the Torah as the source of Jewish law. They studied in depth the meaning of every passage—indeed every word. Since the basis of Jewish law and custom is found in the Torah, it is the starting point for the exploration of the laws of the ceremony of the *Bris.* Analysis of this passage from the Book of Genesis will make clear the origin and the significance of the *Bris.*

THIS IS MY COVENANT WHICH
YE SHALL KEEP

The word *Bris* itself is a Hebrew word which means "covenant" or "agreement." The circumcision ceremony is a sign of this covenant that began with Abraham, the first Hebrew, who was commanded to circumcise his son, Isaac. The circumcision is a symbol of Abraham's pledge to God that he would observe His ways and follow His precepts. Just as Abraham made this agreement, so the Jews, by means of the ceremony of circumcision, accept this *Bris,* or covenant, from generation to generation. They induct their sons into this same covenant and trust that Judaism will continue through them. The *Bris* is performed as a religious act, not merely as a surgical operation.

EVERY MALE AMONG YOU SHALL BE CIRCUMCISED

This sign of Jewishness is incumbent upon all males. The rule is definite, and has been observed by Jews almost continually since the time of Abraham. As such, it is one of the oldest rites in the Jewish ritual.

AND HE THAT IS EIGHT DAYS OLD SHALL BE CIRCUMCISED AMONG YOU

The Torah indicates specifically, and leaves no room for interpretation, that the *Bris* take place on the eighth day. The *Bris* is held, therefore, on the eighth day, whether this be a weekday, the Sabbath, Rosh HaShanah or even Yom Kippur. The eighth day is determined by starting with the day of birth as the first day. A baby born on a Thursday morning will have his *Bris* the following Thursday; a baby born on Monday will have his *Bris* the following Monday.

It must be remembered that, according to Jewish tradition, a new day starts at sunset; thus, a baby born on Thursday evening, after sunset, will be circumcised a week later on Friday.

The Rabbis noted the words "the eighth day" and have interpreted this to mean that the ceremony must take place during the daytime and not at night. Also, the *Bris* is generally performed early in the morning, since Jews always try to perform their *Mitzvos* (religious ordinances) as soon as it is possible to do so.

A *Bris* is postponed only if the health of the child requires it. Under such circumstances, or when a child is delivered by Caesarean section, the *Bris* is never held on the Sabbath or on a Jewish holiday.

A child is considered Jewish if he is born of a Jewish mother. The *Bris* itself, then, does not make the child Jewish, but it is a significant sign of the entrance of the child into the Jewish way of life.

THE IMPORTANCE OF THE *BRIS* TO JUDAISM

The *Bris*, called *Os HaBris* (sign of the covenant), has always been zealously observed by Jews, even under the most adverse conditions, as a means of perpetuating their faith and its ideals. It was no wonder then that Baruch Spinoza, the famous philosopher, said that as long as Jews continue the rite of circumcision, they will exist. The *Bris* serves as a bond of unity for the preservation of the Jewish people.

Whenever the observance of the *Bris* did waver, leaders of the Jewish community reminded the people of its importance. The prophet, Ezekiel, emphasized the *Bris* when he pointed out to the Jews that the Babylonians and the Assyrians among whom they were living did not practice circumcision and that this distinguishing rite was essential to Jewish survival.

The first great crisis in connection with the *Bris* occurred during the reign of the cruel Antiochus Epiphanes, and is recorded in the Book of the Maccabees. Although Antiochus prohibited the *Bris,* Jews, at the risk of their lives, persisted and continued its observance.

When Christianity was still a sect of Judaism, Paul, preaching to the Gentiles, allowed conversion to his religion without the ceremony of the *Bris*. Afterwards, he preached abandonment of the rite for all. It was the exclusion of the *Bris* from the practice of the Christian sect, that was one of the precipitating factors in the break between Judaism and Christianity.

The Roman Emperor Hadrian (135 C.E.) issued an edict which prohibited the mutilation of any part of the body, violation of which was punishable by death. This edict was applied to the Jews observing the *Bris*. Nevertheless, though under pain of death, they persisted in the observance of this rite, so crucial did they consider it to the existence of Judaism.

THE CEREMONY OF THE *BRIS*

In days of yore, the *Bris* usually was held in the synagogue immediately after the *Shacharis* (morning) service. It was the function of the *Kvater* and the *Kvaterin* (Godfather and Godmother) to bring the child from his home to the synagogue door. A man, appointed by the father of the boy, was designated the *Sandek*. It was his privilege to carry the lad from the door of the synagogue and to hold him during the course of the *Bris*. The word *Sandek* is derived from the Greek and means "with child."

Every synagogue had a special chair, called the "Chair of Elijah," on which the child was placed for the circumcision. It seems that the "Chair of Elijah" and mention of the prophet Elijah in connection with the *Bris* is a late addition to Jewish tradition, probably post-Talmudic. It is recorded in the First Book of Kings (19:10–14), that Elijah complained bitterly that the Jews would surely become assimilated and disappear since they had forsaken God's covenant, the observance of the *Bris*. Because of Elijah's lack of faith in the Jewish people, God commanded that he be present in spirit whenever the Holy Covenant was entered into by newborn Israelites. The Rabbis commented that the tongue which testified that Israel had forsaken the covenant now witnesses the keeping of the covenant; Elijah was to be present at all circumcisions.

Although this reference in the First Book of Kings may be the only direct connection between Elijah and the *Bris,* the prophet Elijah has other virtues commonly attributed to him which may also connect him, however indirectly, with the *Bris.* The prophet Elijah symbolizes faith and hope for the future, and the ultimate redemption of the Jewish people. No wonder then that he is mentioned as the protector of the boy at his *Bris.* Elijah is mentioned to express the hope that the lad may come under Elijah's protection and live in an era of peace and tranquillity.

Today, although the *Bris* is held in the home or at the hospital, we still appoint a *Kvater* and *Kvaterin,* their positions now being honorary. The *Sandek* still holds the baby during the circumcision. At present, the pillow placed on the table for the circumcision is termed the "Chair of Elijah."

THE *MOHEL*

It is the basic duty of the father to welcome his son into the fold by circumcising him. Today, the father appoints a competent *Mohel* to do this for him. Traditionally, a *minyan* (meaning literally "count"—a quorum of ten men necessary for public worship and ceremonies) is required, but in view of the fact that the *Bris* is considered the personal responsibility of a father to his son, rather than a public ceremony, a *minyan,* although advisable, is not necessary.

Mohalim (plural of *Mohel*) today are certified by some individuals or groups. In the New York area, *Mohalim* are certified by the Milah Board of New York. To be qualified to serve as a *Mohel*, a man must be an observant Jew, not necessarily a Rabbi, who has been trained in the surgical procedure of circumcision as well as the details of Jewish law in relation to the *Bris*. A *Mohel* may be regarded as a specialist in his field and is preeminently qualified to perform the *Bris Milah*. In fact, Queen Elizabeth of England chose the chief *Mohel* of London to perform the circumcision on her son, Prince Charles, as she felt that he was most qualified.

SEUDAS MITZVAH

The *Seudas Mitzvah* (feast celebrating the observance of a *mitzvah*) is held at the conclusion of the *Bris* ceremony. The *Seudas Mitzvah* is also held after such ceremonies as the *Pidyon HaBen* (Redemption of the First Born) and the wedding. This feast is considered an integral part of the religious event and, therefore, should certainly be a feast conforming to the Jewish dietary laws.

THE *BRIS* SERVICE

Today, most *Bris* ceremonies take place in the home. The rite begins as the *Kvater* and the *Kvaterin* bring the baby into the room. The baby is handed over to the *Sandek* whose task it is to hold the baby.

As the baby is brought in, those present say:

"Blessed be he who is coming!"

This is a customary greeting, not one used exclusively at a *Bris*.

The father of the child then says:

I am ready to perform the positive *mitzvah* that the Almighty, Blessed be He, ordained, that I shall circumcise my son, as it is written in the Torah, "And he that is eight days old shall be circumcised among you, every male throughout your generations." (Genesis 17:12)

It should be noted, once again, that prior to the performance of the circumcision, the law from the Torah is quoted. The *Bris* is one of the affirmative *mitzvos* of the six hundred and thirteen incumbent on a male Jew.

The *Mohel* then continues:

"This is the chair of Elijah, may he be remembered for good."

In mentioning the Chair of Elijah, the *Mohel* points to the table or the chair on which the circumcision will take place. The prophet Elijah, remembered for faith and for hope in the future, is recalled. May the baby's life be a good one, in which peace and righteousness prevail.

The *Mohel* recites:

I wait for Thy salvation, O Lord. (Genesis 49:18)

I have hoped for Thy salvation, O Lord,
And have done Thy commandments. (Psalms 119:166)

I rejoice at Thy word
As one that findeth great spoil. (Psalms 119:162)

Great peace have they that love Thy law;
And there is no stumbling for them. (Psalms 119:165)

Happy is the man whom Thou choosest, and bringest near,
That he may dwell in Thy courts . . . (Psalms 65:5)

Here the *Mohel* quotes from various books of the Bible, mostly from the Psalms. All of these passages reflect the great spiritual joy of this happy religious celebration.

The *Mohel* then recites the following blessing prior to performing the *Bris:*

"Blessed art Thou, O Lord our God, King of the universe, who has sanctified us with Thy commandments and commanded us concerning the circumcision."

Here, as in all instances of the performance of a *mitzvah,* the appropriate blessing is recited, immediately before the performance of the commandment.

After the circumcision, the father recites the following blessing:

"Blessed art Thou, O Lord our God, King of the universe, who has sanctified us with Thy commandments and has commanded us to enter our sons into the covenant of Abraham our father."

Those present at the *Bris* respond:

"Just as this child has now entered into the covenant, so may he enter into the study of Torah, *Chupah* (nuptial canopy) and into good deeds."

Those present wish the boy the best that life has to offer:

a) A life crowned with the study of Torah—study of Torah gives the lad a knowledge of Judaism and a faith in God. The ways of the Lord will enrich his life and give it meaning.

b) *Chupah* (the nuptial canopy—symbolizing marriage)—May he have a life which will possess marital happiness. Through his marriage, no matter how far it may seem to be in the future, may Judaism be handed on, through his children, to the next generation.

c) Good Deeds—Judaism believes that it is not only the relationship between man and God that is important, but also the relationship between man and man. May the boy perform many good deeds of honesty, justice, kindness and mercy throughout his life. The wish for the boy is for a full life in conformity with God's ways. Hope for material success is not mentioned. Wealth does not necessarily bring true happiness.

The *Mohel* then takes a cup filled with wine and continues:

"Blessed art Thou, O Lord our God, King of the universe, who bringest forth the fruit of the vine."

Many religious events are marked with the blessing over the wine. This blessing is recited as part of the *Kiddush* (prayer of sanctification) which is chanted every Sabbath and holiday. The blessing is also part of the *Pidyon HaBen* (Redemption of the first born) as well as the wedding service. Wine, for Jews, is a symbol of life, joy,

Torah, Israel and Jerusalem. In Jewish literature all of these precious concepts have been compared to the sweet taste of wine.

The *Mohel* then continues:

Blessed art Thou, O Lord our God, King of the universe, who has sanctified the beloved from birth, setting your statute in his flesh (the *Bris*) and sealing it with your holy covenant. Therefore, O living God, our Portion and our Rock, give command to deliver from destruction Thy dearly beloved people for the sake of the covenant Thou hast set in our flesh. Blessed art Thou, O Lord, who dost establish Thy covenant.

The Jews have traditionally entered their sons into the Covenant of God through this rite of circumcision.

The *Mohel,* or Rabbi, continues and offers the following prayer in behalf of the child as he is officially named:

Our God and God of our fathers, preserve this child to his father and mother, and may his name be called in Israel ___(first name of child)___ the son of ___(name of the father)___.

Let the father rejoice in his offspring and the mother be glad with the fruit of her body; as it is written:

Let thy father and thy mother be glad,
And let her that bore thee rejoice.
                    (Proverbs 23:25)

And it is said:

And when I passed by thee, and saw thee
wallowing in thy blood, I said unto thee:
In thy blood live; yea, I said unto thee:

In thy blood, live; (by the blood of
circumcision).

(Ezekiel 16:6)

And it is said:

He hath remembered His covenant for ever,
The word which He commanded to a thousand generations;
(The covenant) which He made with Abraham,
And His oath unto Isaac;
And He established it unto Jacob for a statute,
To Israel for an everlasting covenant.

(Psalms 105:8–10)

And it is said:

And Abraham circumcised his son Isaac when
he was eight days old, as God had commanded him.

(Genesis 21:4)

O give thanks unto the Lord, for He is good,
For His mercy endureth for ever.

(Psalms 118:1)

The forgoing section of the service consists of a series of passages from the Bible citing references to the *Bris* as well as passages of joy over the blessing of this happy event.

The service then continues:

This little child ___(name of child is inserted here)___ May he grow up. Just as he has now entered into the covenant, so may he enter into Torah, the *Chupah* and into good deeds.

A few drops of wine are given to the baby and the *Mohel* or Rabbi blesses the child.

NAMING THE GIRL

It is customary to name the girl in the synagogue when the Torah is read. The father of the newborn girl is called to the Torah. Immediately after his *Aliyah,* the following prayer is recited:

May He who has blessed our fathers, Abraham, Isaac and Jacob, Sarah, Rebekah, Rachel and Leah, also bless   (mother's first name)   the daughter of   (name of mother's father) and her newly born daughter with good fortune and let her name be called in Israel   (girl's name)   daughter of   (first name of father)   for which the husband and father blesses them and offers charity in their behalf. Because of this may the parents be privileged to raise her to attain the three-fold blessing of Torah, *Chupah* (nuptial canopy) and good deeds.

Just as God blessed the three fathers, Abraham, Isaac and Jacob, and the four mothers, Sarah, Rebekah, Rachel and Leah, so may He also bring blessing to the mother and to the newborn daughter. When invoking the "God of our Fathers" Jews declare themselves as loyal children adoring the same God.

In this prayer, it should be noted that the father promises to donate charity. It is a Jewish custom to give to charity at times when one petitions God's favor. The Hebrew word for charity is *Tzedakah* which literally means "righteousness." Through performing the merciful act of charity, it is hoped that God will grant the petition.

CHAPTER THREE

PIDYON HABEN
(REDEMPTION OF THE FIRST-BORN)

The Jews, like most religious and cultural groups of the world, had special rites for the first-born. The first-born of any species, man or beast, was offered to God. While most nations of the world offered their first-born by sacrificial slaying, the Jews consecrated their first-born, endowing them with leadership and looking to them for counsel.

The first-born son received the birthright, which made him the head of the entire family or clan, the spiritual leader and the owner of the family's material possessions. In the Bible, we read that Abraham passed on the mantle of leadership to his only son, Isaac. Isaac married Rebekah and she gave birth to twins, Esau and Jacob, Esau being the first-born. It was clear, however, that Esau's personality was unsuited to the spiritual and moral aspects of his father's beliefs. But since he was the elder, he was to inherit the material possessions, as well as the mantle of spiritual leadership. And so, when Isaac was old, he called for Esau to give him the blessing of the first-born. Jacob, with his mother's help, tricked both his brother and his father and obtained the birthright in his brother's place. Jacob became the spiritual heir and carried on the family's belief in one God.

The first-born also play an important role in the exodus of the Israelites from Egypt. Since the time of the tenth plague when the first-born in all of Egypt were slain and only the Israelite homes were spared, the first-born were to be consecrated to God. This situation seems to have changed when the Jews started their wanderings in the desert, after the exodus from Egypt. As soon as the Tabernacle was constructed in the desert, Aaron and his sons were designated as priests to offer sacrifices and to serve in the Tabernacle. Thus the responsibility for the spiritual leadership no longer lay with the first-born, but was instead passed on to the priests. The ceremony of the *Pidyon HaBen* (redemption of the first-born) symbolizes this transferral of leadership from the first-born to the *Kohen* (priest) as is stipulated in the Torah.

Today, the spiritual leader of the Jewish people is the Rabbi, although this role is of late origin and is certainly not Biblical. The leadership of the Jewish people has thus

been democratized, in that it is not restricted to the eldest
son or to a particular priestly family. Any worthy male
Jew desiring to study may now be ordained as a Rabbi
and assume a position of leadership.

Some of the laws of the *Pidyon HaBen* as stated in the
Torah are:

Sanctify unto Me all the first-born, whatsoever openeth the
womb among the children of Israel, both of man and of beast,
it is Mine.

(Exodus 13:2)

All the first-born of thy sons thou shalt redeem.

(Exodus 34:20)

And their redemption money—from a month old shalt thou
redeem them—shall be, according to thy valuation, five shekels of silver, after the shekel of the sanctuary—the same is
twenty gerahs.

(Numbers 18:16)

And I, behold, I have taken the Levites from among the children of Israel . . . and the Levites shall be Mine; for all the
first-born are Mine: on the day that I smote all the first-born
in the land of Egypt I hallowed unto Me all the first-born in
Israel, both man and beast, Mine they shall be: I am the Lord.

(Numbers 3:12, 13)

From these statements, we may deduce the following
laws of redemption:
1. "Sanctify unto Me all the first-born . . . the first-born
of thy sons shalt thou give unto Me. . . . All the first-born
of thy sons thou shalt redeem . . ." These passages indi-

cate the consecration of the first-born to God as well as the ordained redemption from this responsibility.

2. The Torah stipulates the first-born to be that which "openeth the womb." Therefore, a son born of a woman who previously had a miscarriage, would not have a *Pidyon HaBen;* nor would a son born to a woman who had a previous still birth. Since a child born by Caesarean section does not come from the "opening of the womb," he also would not have a *Pidyon HaBen.*

According to the Torah, it is the first-born son of every mother that shall be redeemed. A man having a second wife could conceivably participate in two ceremonies if both his first and second wives gave birth to sons as their first-born while married to him.

It is the father's responsibility to redeem his son. He must do so, and can, even if he is in a city distant from that in which his son is born. If the father dies before the *Pidyon HaBen,* the boy may redeem himself when he gets older.

3. "From a month old shalt thou redeem them." The *Pidyon HaBen* takes place after the first month of life. The statement "from one month" implies that the redemption cannot take place before thirty days have elapsed. As Jews wish to observe the *Mitzvos* (religious ordinances) as soon as possible, the redemption takes place on the thirty-first day.

The *Pidyon HaBen* should be held on the thirty-first day and should not be postponed. Since no surgical operation is necessary, as in the case of the *Bris,* the *Pidyon*

HaBen should take place on the thirty-first day, even if the *Bris* has not yet taken place because of the health of the child.

A *Pidyon HaBen* does not take place on the Sabbath or on festivals, but does take place on *Chol HaMoed* (the intermediate days) of Sukkos and Passover.

The reasoning of the Rabbis in postponing the *Pidyon HaBen* if the thirty-first day fall on the Sabbath or on a festival, while scheduling the *Bris* even if it fall on the Sabbath, illustrates the reverence that the Rabbis felt for the Torah. In connection with the *Bris*, the Torah indicates: "And he that is eight days old shall be circumcised." The eighth day is specifically named, and no alternatives are allowed. Thus the *Bris* must be held on the Sabbath or on a festival. When speaking of the *Pidyon HaBen*, the Torah states: "*From* a month old shalt thou redeem him." Since the rule here is a little more indefinite, the Rabbis allowed themselves the leeway of postponing the *Pidyon HaBen* beyond the thirty-first day, if that day were a Sabbath or a festival.

4. "And their redemption money . . . five shekels of silver." It is customary for the father to pay the *Kohen* five silver dollars to redeem his son. The Torah stipulates five shekels, which was a coin of intrinsic value. Five silver dollars are used today since they are coins of definite value, as opposed to the symbolic value of a dollar bill.

The *Kohen*, receiving the five silver dollars during the ceremony, should return the coins to the father or donate them to charity. The reason for this is that the Torah stipulates that the redemption must take place on one hand, and we are not sure exactly who is a *Kohen* on the other. Today we have no written record—no genealogy to prove that an individual is indeed a *Kohen*, and must simply accept the individual's word. Since redemption is obligatory, the *Kohen* redeems; but lest unbeknown to himself, he not be a *Kohen*, he should return the coins.

5. "And I have taken the Levites from among the Children of Israel instead of every first-born." The Torah here indicates the assignment of the Levites to the responsibility of the first-born. For this reason, the sons of the *Kohanim* and the *Leviim* are exempt from the *Pidyon HaBen*. For the purpose of the *Pidyon HaBen*, even if the mother of the child is the daughter of a *Kohen* or a Levite, the child need not have a *Pidyon HaBen*.

THE CEREMONY OF THE *PIDYON HABEN*

A cup of wine, a *challah* and a pillow for the child are placed on the table. The child is brought in and placed on the pillow for the ceremony. The service is basically a dialogue between the father of the child and the *Kohen*.

The father says:

"This is my first-born son, the first-born of his mother, and the Holy One, Blessed be He, has given command to redeem him."

The father here starts the dialogue by stating the reason for the *Pidyon HaBen*.

The father then places five silver dollars before the *Kohen* as the *Kohen* asks the father:

"Which would you rather do, give me your first-born son, who is the first-born of his mother, or redeem him for five shekalim, as is stipulated in the Torah?"

The *Kohen* indicates that the redemption is ordained in the Torah and stipulates the amount needed for the redemption.

The father then answers:

"I desire to redeem my son and here is the money of redemption as is stipulated in the Torah."

Since the father is about to perform a *mitzvah* (religious ordinance or commandment), he recites the appropriate blessing before fulfilling the particular commandment.

Blessed art Thou, O Lord, our God, King of the universe, who has sanctified us with Thy commandments and commanded us concerning the redemption of the first-born son.

The father and mother then pronounce the *she-he-che-ya-nu* blessing, in which they thank God for having sustained them and preserved them so that they may celebrate this joyous occasion.

"Blessed art Thou, O Lord, our God, King of the universe, who has kept us in life and preserved us and enabled us to reach this milestone in our lives."

This *she-he-che-ya-nu* blessing is used not only for the various milestones of life, but also several times during the year. On Rosh HaShanah, Yom Kippur, Sukkos and other festivals, the Jew thanks God that he has lived to celebrate that holiday once again. Jews consider life as an ever-renewing gift from God, and continually express their appreciation for God's beneficence.

The *Kohen* then blesses the child:

May it be Thy will, O our Father, who is in heaven, that as this child has been privileged to undergo redemption, so may he be privileged to fulfill all the commandments in the Torah.

God make thee as Ephraim and as Manasseh.

(Genesis 48:20)

The Lord bless thee, and keep thee;
The Lord make His face to shine upon thee, and be gracious unto thee;
The Lord lift up His countenance upon thee, and give thee peace.

(Numbers 6:24–26)

"God make thee as Ephraim and Manasseh." This is a passage from the Book of Genesis and is a part of the blessings Jacob bestows on his children before he dies. Joseph, Jacob's son, who occupied a high office in the Egyptian government, brought his own two sons to his father for his blessing. Jacob, in additon to blessing his own sons, also blesses Joseph's sons, Ephraim and Manasseh. By doing so, he granted to Joseph twice the inheritance received by any of his brothers.

"May the Lord make thee as Ephraim and Manasseh" is

the prayer which the Jewish father uses to bless his sons every Friday evening. Ephraim and Manasseh could have been granted exalted positions in the Egyptian government, similar to the position held by their father, Joseph. Instead, they chose to cast their lot with the Jewish people. The *Kohen* here prays that the child may show the same loyalty to the Jewish people as did Ephraim and Manasseh of old.

The *Kohen* then continues with the following words:

> The Lord is thy keeper;
> The Lord is thy shade upon thy right hand.
> > (Psalms 121:5)

> For length of days, and years of life,
> And peace, will they add to thee.
> > (Proverbs 3:2)

> The Lord shall keep thee from all evil;
> He shall keep thy soul.
> > (Psalms 121:7)

These passages at the conclusion of the ceremony express the hope that the Lord will protect the boy during his lifetime, grant him the blessing of peace and guard him from evil.

The ceremony is concluded with the blessing over the cup of wine and the *challah*. This begins the *Seudas Mitzvah*, the feast celebrating the fulfillment of the joyous commandment.

CHAPTER FOUR

BAR MITZVAH   BAS MITZVAH   CONFIRMATION

BAR MITZVAH

The ceremony of *Bar Mitzvah,* for boys at the age of thirteen celebrating the assumption of their religious obligations, is a comparatively new ritual in Judaism. The rites of the *Bris,* the *Pidyon HaBen,* marriage and mourning have their basis in the Torah and *Talmud.* Since the *Bar Mitzvah* has no basis in these sources, it is the least rooted of all the milestones in the life of the Jew. Before the thirteenth or the fourteenth century, there was no *Bar Mitzvah* ritual for boys at the age of thirteen. The origin of this ceremony is indeed obscure.

36

The Bible seems to consider twenty as the age of responsibility, although no ceremony is recorded when one reaches the age of twenty. In Exodus (30:14), we read of a census that was taken among the Israelites. Only those twenty years of age or older were to be counted. In Leviticus (27:1–5), the valuation of individuals for the redemption of vows to God was determined according to age. Individuals between the ages of five and twenty were grouped together in valuation, giving some indication that maturity comes at the age of twenty. Additional evidence is found in Numbers (1:3–20), where only those above the age of twenty were considered available for military duty.

The *Talmud* is also silent with regard to a *Bar Mitzvah* at the age of thirteen, indicating that this ceremony was unknown in Talmudic days. The *Talmud*, however, does use the word *Bar Mitzvah* twice. Both times the reference is to any Jew who observes the commandments, not necessarily to a boy at age thirteen. The *Talmud* does stipulate that the age of thirteen is the age at which a boy assumes legal responsibility. In referring to a boy of thirteen, the *Talmud* does not use the words *Bar Mitzvah*, but *Bar Onshin* (one who is punishable); for at thirteen, the child becomes liable for any wrongdoing he may commit. On the other hand, the *Talmud* indicates that a man must be twenty years old to inherit real estate or to serve as a judge.

The *Midrash Rabbah*, commenting on the twenty-fifth chapter of Genesis, verse twenty-seven, relates the story of the growth and education of the two brothers, Jacob and Esau. For thirteen years, both Jacob and Esau went to school and returned from school; afterwards, Jacob went to school and Esau went to foreign shrines. Rabbi Eleazar, son of Rabbi Simeon, commented that a man is responsible for his son's education till the age of thirteen. Thereafter, the father is free of this duty. However, this reference makes no mention of a *Bar Mitzvah* ceremony, or of the assumption of religious responsibilities not previously granted.

Although the *Ethics of the Fathers* (a part of the *Talmud*) indicates "at thirteen the age is reached for the fulfillment of *mitzvos*" (Chapter 5, Mishnah 24), boys would observe the various *mitzvos* that are associated today with *Bar Mitzvah*, such as being called to the Torah and putting on te*phillin* (phylacteries) well before the age of thirteen. The *Talmud* (Megillah 23a) teaches that a minor may be called to the Torah for an *aliyah* (honor of being called to make a blessing at the time that the Torah is read). Maimonides (1135–1204) indicates that when a boy is mature enough to understand the significance of the rituals involved, he may be called to the Torah, even before the age of thirteen. It is known that until the fourteenth century, a minor was taught to put on *tephillin* by his father as soon as he was able to understand their significance and know how to take care of them properly. Some authorities also seem to hold that the young boy, when knowledgeable, may be counted in the *minyan* (quorum of ten males required for a religious service). It appears, therefore, that the age of thirteen was probably the maximum age for the assumption of one's religious duties.

Certainly, if the *Bar Mitzvah* were known prior to the fourteenth century, there would be a discussion of the rules for *Bar Mitzvah*, if not in the Torah, then surely in the *Talmud* or in the later writings. Yet the *Gaonim* (authorities on Jewish law from the sixth to the eleventh centuries), Rabbi Isaac Alfasi (eleventh century), and Maimonides (twelfth century) mentioned neither a *Bar Mitzvah* nor any other ceremony to be observed at the age of thirteen. No ceremony, as such, was really needed, for the young boy could be called to the Torah, put on *tephillin* (phylacteries) and was even induced to begin fasting on Yom Kippur before the age of thirteen.

DEVELOPMENT OF THE *BAR MITZVAH* CEREMONY

Jews always believed in an intensive religious education for their children. One of the most well-known prayers in the Jewish liturgy, called the *Shema,* citing a passage from the Torah (Deuteronomy 6:7), exclaims: "Thou shalt teach them (the commandments) diligently unto thy children." Throughout the ages, the child was most carefully taught and, through education, brought closer to the synagogue and religious services.

It seems that boys were brought to the synagogue at

about the age of four years. At least, stories may be found in Jewish literature relating to complaints that these children made noise at the services. Parents wanted to accustom their children to synagogue attendance. A later practice permitted the children to sip the *Kiddush* wine at the service. Children also participated in the observance of *Simchas Torah* by carrying flags, being called to the Torah and being served with sweets on this day.

The child was later expected to attend the services more regularly and to learn how to pray with the congregation. The Rabbis, however, understood that there were in the congregation children, women, or unlearned men who would not be able to follow the Torah readings. The *Tractate Sopherim* states, for example, that after the reading of the Torah in Hebrew, it was translated into the vernacular for the benefit of those who could not understand the Hebrew.

The *Tractate Sopherim* also indicates that a child, at the age of nine or ten years, was initiated into the observance of Yom Kippur by fasting for a few hours. However, the Rabbis were most cautious to see that this was not overdone. One of the sages, Rabbi Acha, used to tell his congregation after the *Musaf* service: "My brethren, let every one of you who has a child go home and make him eat. . . ."

Until approximately the thirteenth or fourteenth century, boys before the age of thirteen naturally attended services but those who were judged mature and reached an acceptable level of learning were called to the Torah and were privileged to put on *tephillin* (phylacteries). However, in the thirteenth century, the level of Talmudic learning amongst German Jews as well as elsewhere degenerated. No longer were boys considered responsible enough to don *tephillin* or knowledgeable enough to be called to the Torah prior to the maximum age of thirteen years. The first scholar to have used the term *Bar Mitzvah,* in the modern-day sense, was Mordecai ben Hillel, a German *Halachist* of the thirteenth century. All other references to the *Bar Mitzvah* appear after this date.

It was on the Sabbath after the boy's thirteenth Hebrew birthday that the *Bar Mitzvah* took place. He was called to the Torah for the first time, often for the *maftir aliyah* (the honor of being called to the Torah with the additional honor of chanting a portion from the Prophets). When the boy finished his *aliyah,* his father would rise and say:

"Baruch she-pet-rani me-onsho shel zeh
Blessed be He, who has freed me from this responsibility."

The father declared that he was no longer responsible for his son's Jewish education and for seeing to it that his son observed the *mitzvos* (religious ordinances) of Judaism. Two interpretations have been given for this statement: (a) The father thanks God for removing from him the responsibility for any sins that his son might commit; (b) the humble father declares that no longer will his son suffer for his own failings in teaching him.

The proud parents provided a *seudah* (meal) for relatives and friends after the service. The meal was a simple one and was followed by a *derashah* (sermon) by the *Bar Mitzvah* boy in which he showed what he had learned.

Soon after the advent of the *Bar Mitzvah*, the *seudah* or party began to become more elaborate, rivaling in importance the actual religious ceremony. In 1595, in Cracow, a communal tax was placed on the *Bar Mitzvah* feast so as to keep it within the bounds of good taste.

BAR MITZVAH TODAY

Due to the fact that the *Bar Mitzvah* is not rooted in our ancient tradition, there appears to be no great uniformity in the role of the *Bar Mitzvah* in the synagogue service. Generally, the boy participates in the synagogue service on the Sabbath after his thirteenth birthday, calculated according to the Jewish calendar (which may fall as much as several weeks before or after his English birthday). Boys who have lost either parent are eligible for *Bar Mitzvah* after their twelfth birthday. The Rabbis felt that the loss of a parent gave the child earlier maturity, so they deemed them responsible to assume their religious majority at twelve years of age.

Before a boy's thirteenth Hebrew birthday, he is not eligible to lead the congregation during a religious service. Leading the congregation in prayer is a privilege given to any male Jew above the age of thirteen, and is not restricted to a Cantor or a Rabbi. The first time that the boy participates in the service is indeed a milestone in his life and is a joyous occasion for the entire family. The boy's role in the religious service may vary; most of the time he will chant the *haftorah* (a chapter from the prophetic writings). At times he may chant the entire section of the Torah designated for that Sabbath, or he may lead the congregation in worship. Most *B'nai Mitzvah* (plural of *Bar Mitzvah*) take place, as we have stated, at the Saturday morning service following the boy's thirteenth birthday. The fact that the Saturday morning service is the major service of the week, has made this service a favorite one in which to include the *Bar Mitzvah* ceremony. A boy may, however, participate in the service whenever the Torah is read in the synagogue—on Monday or Thursday mornings, or on *Rosh Chodesh* (the beginning of a new Hebrew month). It is the fervent hope of the family and the congregation that just as the lad now assumes his role as an adult Jew, so may he become a credit to the House of Israel as he matures.

BAS MITZVAH

A twentieth-century arrival on the Jewish scene is the ceremony of *Bas Mitzvah,* whose origin has generally been ascribed to Dr. Mordecai M. Kaplan. As such, of course, it is a new milestone in the life of the Jew, and its basis would not be found in our traditional sources of law.

It represents a widespread desire to grant equal recognition to the girl for her religious studies. Indeed, it might also be regarded an extension of the idea of equal rights for women, a salient characteristic of twentieth-century thought.

The amount of recognition granted to the girl varies from synagogue to synagogue. Some Conservative synagogues have granted girls equality with boys and hold the *Bas Mitzvah* on Saturday morning, permit the girl to have an *aliyah* at the Torah and to chant the *haftorah* as well. The Rabbinical Assembly Committee on Jewish Law and Standards issued a majority report in 1955 permitting *aliyos* for women under certain circumstances. Those synagogues providing the Saturday morning *Bas Mitzvah* have introduced into their services something new to the Conservative movement.

Most Conservative congregations have not, as yet, adopted *Bas Mitzvah* during the Saturday morning service, and consequently grant their "equality" for girls by having their *Bas Mitzvah* ceremonies at various other times. The Friday evening service is the most popular time for the *Bas Mitzvah*. During the Friday evening service, the girl will often chant a *haftorah*, but not necessarily the one assigned for reading on that Sabbath.

Whatever form the *Bas Mitzvah* takes, whether it be on a Friday evening, Saturday morning or at another time, whether the girl chant a *haftorah* or not, whether she become *Bas Mitzvah* individually or in a group, the *Bas Mitzvah* acknowledges the greater understanding of her role as a Jewess that her education and religious training have given her, and grants her equal status with the male. The *Bas Mitzvah* certainly motivates the girl to undertake formal religious studies in an era when our knowledge of Judaism is found wanting. Jews have always understood the importance of knowledge for women—for they are the ones who instill the love of faith in the hearts of the coming generation. *Bas Mitzvah* has been most successful in implementing this objective.

CONFIRMATION

The ceremony of Confirmation is one in which a group of teenagers confirm their acceptance of Judaism and thus mark a milestone in their Jewish learning. As such, it is a newcomer to the Jewish scene, and therefore is not based on any traditional source such as the Torah, the *Talmud,* or the Codes. Confirmation, as we know it in Judaism, was adapted from the ritual of the Protestant Lutheran church by the Reform movement in Judaism, in the nineteenth century.

Originally, it was for boys only and it was a substitute for the *Bar Mitzvah*. The first known Confirmation took place in Cassel, Westphalia in 1810. As early as 1817 a Reform congregation in Germany confirmed both boys and girls. It is curious to note that the first ceremony in

Cassel could not be held in the synagogue as there was too much opposition to it. The opposition protested, claiming that Confirmation was un-Jewish since children were Jewish by birth and therefore no ceremony was needed.

Prior to the advent of the *Bas Mitzvah,* many Conservative and Orthodox synagogues used the ceremony of Confirmation exclusively for girls, in recognition of the fact that girls were now receiving a formal Jewish education. In bygone days, formal Jewish education was exclusively for boys. The girl received her Jewish education at home. Today, as Jewish observance in the home has decreased, it is necessary for girls as well as boys to attend a Religious School.

Now that many synagogues have instituted the *Bas Mitzvah,* a new meaning has been given to the Confirmation ceremony. It has become increasingly apparent that a strong foundation in Judaism cannot be given to the child in the time spent in Religious School prior to the *Bar* or *Bas Mitzvah.* In order to motivate the youngster to continue beyond this stage of learning for two or more additional years, the Confirmation of both boys and girls is being set at the age of fifteen or sixteen, and a new milestone is being established for those who have truly received a realistic basic Jewish education. This is a wonderful example of how Judaism has adapted a ceremony to mark a worthwhile goal.

Since Confirmation is not based in Jewish tradition, each congregation and its Rabbi have set their own rules for qualification for the ceremony, the nature of the ceremony and when it shall take place. One of the most favored holidays for Confirmation is Shavuos, selected because it comes at the end of the school year and because the holiday of Shavuos commemorates the acceptance of the Torah by the Israelites at Mount Sinai. The young people being confirmed symbolically accept the tenets of the Jewish people, now that they have the basic knowledge and understanding of Judaism.

The rite of Confirmation varies with the synagogue, but usually consists of a presentation in words or music by the Confirmants on the significance of the holiday, Judaism or the value of their Jewish education.

CHAPTER . FIVE

MARRIAGE

THE *MITZVAH* OF MARRIAGE

It is a Jewish belief that marriage is part of the natural way of life; in fact, it was ordained by the Almighty Himself. For we read in the Torah that Adam was alone in the world and "the Lord said: 'It is not good that man should be left alone; I will make a help meet for him' (Genesis 2:18). Adam had the entire world round about him, the sun, the moon and the stars, the animals as well as the plants, but still he was alone. God caused Adam to fall into a deep sleep and from one of Adam's ribs, He created

48

woman. The beautiful Biblical account concludes with the statement, "therefore shall a man leave his father and mother and cleave unto his wife and they shall become one flesh." Together, husband and wife share each other's joys and sorrows as they travel together on the road of life.

Contrast this with the basic Catholic beliefs about marriage which began with the advent of Christianity in the days of Paul. According to Paul, man is composed of two elements, the body and the soul. The body is flesh which is carnal and evil; the soul is holy and pure. Since religion cannot tolerate these carnal desires, those who wish to be holy and pure must curb these bodily physical desires. Only those who were able to do so, could become priests. This is the reason why the priesthood and various religious orders do not countenance marriage. Marriage is for the ordinary person, and is necessary for the propagation of the species.

The Jew believes that both the body and the soul must interact harmoniously for the fullest development of man. One's physical desires are also a creation of God and should be satisfied within the framework of marriage. The highest fulfillment in marriage is the bringing of children into the world, observing the *mitzvah* of *p'ru u'r'vu* (Be fruitful and multiply) (Genesis 9:7). As Noah left the ark, he saw a rainbow stretched across the heavens. At that time, he received the promise from God that never more would He destroy all living creatures on earth. God instructed Noah to "Be fruitful and multiply." Begetting of children, say the Rabbis, is ordained by God. Each married couple satisfies the religious ordinance by having at least one boy and one girl.

Among Jews, the unmarried state is strongly discouraged. In Talmudic days, the rule was that one must be married by the age of eighteen, although scholars studying the Torah were exempted from this rule. So important was marriage, that there are records in which Jewish courts compelled a man to marry, although they never specified whom he should marry.

It is most interesting to study the biographies of the hundreds of great Jewish leaders, Rabbis or other men of renown from the Talmudic days through the entire Middle Ages; one discovers that there were only three men who were never married. They were Ben Azzai, who may have been engaged to Rabbi Akiba's daughter, although the marriage was never held; Isaac Israeli, a Kairowan physicist and scientist of the tenth-century; Yehudah Bar Ilai, a seventh-century physician, philosopher and Talmudist.

The Talmud indicates that one who remains unmarried is considered an incomplete person and lives without joy, without blessing and without good. In fact, a person who remains single is termed a "murderer," in view of the fact that he never fathered children. An unmarried man is called a "lad" no matter how old he may be. Marriage is so important that, although no business may be transacted on the Sabbath, details of a marriage contract may still be discussed.

MATING

Who can really explain the miracle of love and a happy marriage? Jewish tradition credits mating directly to God; for "finding a proper mate is as difficult a feat as was the parting of the Red Sea" (Talmud, Sotah 2a). Have you ever beheld a newly married couple and expressed wonderment over their happiness? Jews use the Yiddish word *beshert*, meaning that the happiness of the marriage was so great, that surely it must have been ordained by heaven.

According to the *Zohar* (a book of mysticism written in the thirteenth-century), a soul descending from heaven is composed of two parts, male and female. The male half enters a male child and the female part enters a female child. The *Zohar*, exalting the concept of marriage, declares that if both the boy and girl are worthy, God will cause them to unite in marriage (*Zohar* iii, 43b).

There is much material in the *Talmud* and other Rabbinic sources, illustrating the belief of Judaism that the hand of God is upon each marriage, and that surely the blessing of a happy married life must be divine. In the *Midrash* (Genesis Rabbah 68.3), a story is told of a Roman matron who, learning that God arranges all marriages, boasted that she could easily do the same. To prove her contention, she proceeded to pair off a thousand of her slaves with a thousand of her handmaidens. The very next morning, the Roman matron was surprised to learn that during the course of the night, quarreling broke out among each of the thousand couples. One had a bruised head, another a wounded arm and, indeed, discord was rampant. Only then did the Roman matron realize that certainly the divine element was necessary in arranging a match.

SELECTING A MATE

Although the Rabbis of the *Talmud* encouraged people to marry, they cautioned individuals to exercise great care in selecting a partner for life. Some of the guide lines presented in the *Talmud* are:

1. Hasten to buy land, but be deliberate in selecting a mate.
2. An old man should not marry a young woman.
3. He who weds for money shall have unworthy offspring.
4. Betroth not a woman you have not seen.
5. Marry not a woman for her money or beauty, for these vanish and damage results.

MONOGAMY IN JUDAISM

Examples of polygamy are found in the Bible and polygamy was practiced in Biblical times. The patriarch Abraham had more than one wife, as did Jacob. Isaac, according to the Bible, had one wife. All of us know the story of King Solomon who had many wives.

But even during the Biblical period, we find the beginning of the move towards monogamy. In Genesis, we read in relation to Adam and Eve: "Therefore, shall man leave his father and mother and shall cleave unto his wife and they shall become one flesh" (Genesis 2:24). This quotation certainly indicates a preference for monogamy. In Deuteronomy (17:17), a king is cautioned not to take many wives so that "his heart not turn away." The prophet Hosea cries out to the people that they should return to worshiping God, and cites the fact that the Children of Israel have a union with God and, therefore, they should be faithful to Him. Surely, if polygamy was countenanced at the time, this illustration could not have been used by the prophet. We know that from the Roman period on, monogamy was practiced.

In the Middle Ages, polygamy, though still permitted in Jewish law, was not practiced. Rabbeinu Gershon, in the early eleventh-century, put a stop to the possibility of polygamy among Jews with his *Takkanah* (edict). This edict was accepted by most European Jews. Some authorities say that this *Takkanah* was to be in effect only till the year 5000, according to the Jewish calendar (1240 C.E.); but most agree that its rule was to apply for all time. It is curious to note that Jews in the Orient and those living in Mohammedan countries did not accept this edict. In certain areas, even today, some Jews, where legally permitted, have taken more than one wife.

PROHIBITED MARRIAGES

The list of close relatives that one is prohibited from marrying is clearly stated in the Book of Leviticus (18:7–17; 20:11–21). A man may not marry his mother, stepmother, mother-in-law, father's or mother's sister, paternal uncle's wife, half sister, stepsister, sister-in-law, wife's sister (as long as his wife is living), daughter-in-law, stepdaughter, granddaughter. Most states of the United States today have laws which prohibit close relatives from marrying very similar to the ones set down in the Torah. According to the Book of Leviticus, first cousins may marry; this is, however, prohibited in many states.

WHEN MAY MARRIAGES BE PERFORMED?

Marriages may be performed on any day of the year with the following exceptions:

1. The Sabbath.
2. Jewish festivals such as Passover, Shavuos, Sukkos, Rosh HaShanah and Yom Kippur. Marriages also may not be performed on *Chol HaMoed* (the middle days of the festival).
3. In the course of Jewish history, the seven weeks between Passover and Shavuos have been marked with

many tragic events. The great Hadrianic persecutions (135 C.E.) took place at this time of the year, as did many massacres of the Jews during the days of the Crusades. Traditionally, it is understood that a severe plague raged among the disciples of Rabbi Akiba at this very time which finally ceased on the 18th day of the Hebrew month of *Iyar,* which is *Lag B'Omer* (the thirty-third day of the counting of the Omer).

Because of the association of these weeks with tragic events in Jewish history, this period has been established as an interval of semi-mourning, during which weddings are curtailed. Customs vary regarding the performance of marriages during *Sephirah* (Counting of the Omer—the period between Passover and Shavuos). The Committee on Jewish Law and Standards of the Rabbinical Assembly, which indicates the viewpoint of the Conservative Movement in Judaism, has ruled that private weddings without music or dancing may take place throughout this period. Marriage without any curtailment of festivity may take place after *Lag B'Omer.* During the first thirty-three days of the *Sephirah,* weddings may take place on *Rosh Chodesh Iyar* (the beginning of the Hebrew month of *Iyar.* The beginning of every month is a semi-holiday to the Jews). Weddings may also take place on Israel Independence Day. The Orthodox movement in Judaism curtails the performance of weddings during the entire seven weeks, except for the special days enumerated.

4. During the three-week period commencing with *Shiva Asar B'Tammuz* (the seventeenth day of the Hebrew

month of Tammuz) and ending with *Tisha B'Av* (the ninth day of the Hebrew month of Av). It was during this period of time that several disasters befell the Jewish people. In the year 586 before the Common Era, the Babylonians who had laid siege to the city of Jerusalem, broke down the walls of the city and destroyed the First Temple. At exactly the same time, according to Jewish tradition, in the year 70 of the Common Era, the Roman army also invaded Jerusalem and then destroyed the Second Temple.

LEVIRATE MARRIAGE

According to the Torah, it is the duty of a man to marry his brother's widow, if that marriage yielded no children. In this way, the deceased brother's name shall not be blotted out, for the first child of this union is considered the child of the deceased. The name Levirate comes from the word "levir" which is the Latin for "brother."

The Torah develops this idea. First, Genesis (38:8) tells about the Levirate marriage where the duty of the man to marry his brother's widow is declared. In addition the responsibility of marrying the widow is extended to the closest relative, should there be no brother. The Book of Deuteronomy states that the responsibility of marrying the deceased man's wife rests only with the brother. When the brother does not wish to consummate this marriage, he may be relieved of this responsibility through the ceremony of *Halitzah*. *Halitzah* is a ceremony in which the man declares that he does not wish to enter into the Levirate marriage and thereby frees the widow of his brother to marry whom she pleases.

In view of the fact that these rules are stated in the Torah, they are basic to our tradition. In modern days, the obligation to perform the Levirate marriage could cause some practical problems. To name but one, the living brother could be married, and therefore, barred by civil law from taking a second wife. Today the *Halitzah* ceremony, as stipulated in the Torah is routinely performed, and one never hears of a Levirate marriage taking place.

MARRIAGE—INTERMARRIAGE

From earliest times, Jews have always considered it important to marry within their own group and faith. We read in the Book of Genesis that Abraham, the first Hebrew, sent his servant Eliezer back to Aram Naharaim to find a wife for his son, Isaac, since Abraham did not want him to marry one who was not of his people.

In the Bible, however, several examples of individuals who did marry outside of their faith can be found. Moses married a foreign woman while he was a fugitive from Egypt. The classic story of an intermarriage is found in the Book of Ruth, where Ruth, a Moabitess, marries a Jew, but her later fidelity to Judaism is well known. In the days of the Kings (950–586 B.C.E.) marriage outside of the fold was common, but these alliances were caused by political conditions and led, ultimately, to the downfall of the kingdom.

In 535 B.C.E., when the bedraggled Jews returned from fifty years of exile in Babylonia, their leaders, Ezra and Nehemiah, cried out to them to preserve Jewish observance and censured intermarriage. Jewish leaders throughout the ages have cautioned Jews against marrying outside their faith. Moses of Coucy, who travelled widely in southern France and Spain in the early part of the thirteenth century, preached to the people against intermarriage. History tells us that he was able to influence some Jews to divorce their non-Jewish wives. The integrity of the Jewish people and its continuity depends on marriage within the faith. Judaism cannot maintain its vitality with mixed marriages.

In our day, Jewish marriages may be performed by a Rabbi only if both the bride and the groom are Jewish. If the non-Jewish partner sincerely wishes to embrace Judaism and goes through the ritual of conversion, a Jewish wedding may be held. Once the conversion has taken place, the partner is considered Jewish, and the marriage is, of course, a marriage of two Jews.

THE WIFE IN JEWISH LAW

The Hebrew term for husband is *Ba'al* while a word for wife is *Be'ulah*. Technically these words mean "master" and "owned one." It should also be noted that marriage ceremonial procedure is much like the formalities surrounding the acquisition of property. Although technically the wife was "owned property," her status was always one which carried the utmost honor, respect and courtesy. Even in the days of the patriarchs, the stories of Sarah and Rebekah and the influence they wielded in their families indicate the status of the wife. A wife is considered a help-meet to her husband. The *Talmud* and other Rabbinic sources are replete with sayings showing the esteem in which the wife is held. The *Talmud* indicates that a man who is married to a virtuous woman will find his life enriched; that a wife is a joy to a man's heart; and that whatever blessing dwells in the house, comes from a wife.

Ancient Judaism was ahead of all contemporary cultures in treating women with the utmost honor and respect. The Jewish husband always protected his wife and provided for her needs. The *Talmud* stipulates that a man may not strike his wife and is liable if he does. The tractate *Baba Metzia* (59a) comments: "A man should always be careful lest he vex his wife; for as her tears come easily, the vexation put upon her comes near to God."

The *Talmud* also specifies that the husband is required to support his wife, provide suitable clothing for her, live with her and fulfill the marital functions, provide for the specified sum as is stipulated in the marriage contract, provide proper medical care for her, provide ransom in case she is kidnapped, arrange a suitable burial, and provide for her from his estate as long as she remains un-married. Many of these obligations are taken for granted today, but Jews were among the first to provide for their women.

In the Bible and in the later sources, we find examples of women who were leaders and were respected in their communities. Leah boasted of the many sons she had borne to Jacob. Hannah, a childless woman, prayed to God for a male child and subsequently gave birth to Samuel. Deborah, a leader in the period of the Judges, was honored for her wise judgment and people sought her out for counsel. In the days of the *Talmud*, Rabbi Meir's wife was noted for her wisdom and is often mentioned in the *Talmud*. Neither the Bible nor later Jewish literature could have made these women heroes, had women, in general, not been considered with respect and courtesy.

The role of women is clearly indicated in the Torah. For the fifth of the Ten Commandments is "Honor thy father and thy mother." Leviticus 19:3 has been interpreted by the Rabbis to provide that respect for one's mother precedes the duty of fearing one's father. Honor and respect for women came early in Judaism. Only a faith that greatly honored its women could have produced this last chapter of the Book of Proverbs:

> A woman of valour who can find?
>   For her price is far above rubies.
> The heart of her husband doth safely trust in her,
>   And he hath no lack of gain.
> She doeth him good and not evil

All the days of her life.
She stretcheth out her hand to the poor;
Yea, she reacheth forth her hands to the needy.
She openeth her mouth with wisdom;
And the law of kindness is on her tongue.
Her children rise up, and call her blessed;
Her husband also, and he praiseth her . . .

Proverbs 31:10–12; 20; 26; 28

MATCH-MAKING IN DAYS OF YORE

Unlike the custom among other peoples, where the women were relegated to the house, Jewish women did have some freedom and were often seen in the streets. In Genesis, we read that Eliezer was sent by Abraham to find a bride for his son, Isaac. Eliezer found the bride, Rebekah, at the well when she went to fetch water. Likewise, Jacob also met Rachel at the well, as she was tending her father's flocks. Although girls did have freedom and were able to meet boys outside of the home, marital arrangements were generally made by the parents.

Even though the Ethics of the Fathers (part of the *Talmud*) indicated that the age of eighteen was the age for marriage, among Jews, as well as among other peoples, marriage often came at an earlier age. The marriage was arranged by the parents of the boy and the girl, but seldom without the approval of the bride and the groom themselves. In the Torah, Rebekah was asked if she wished to marry Isaac. Tacit approval of the bride and the groom was obtained in most instances.

The origin of the dowry is most interesting. At first, the family of the groom or the groom himself had to provide a dowry for the parents of the bride. The reason is clear. Since the girl left her father's house, the bride's family lost a worker; the dowry, therefore, served as compensation for the bride's services. Genesis indicates that Jacob had to work for seven years in order to marry Leah and seven more years for his marriage to Rachel. Gradually the dowry, although symbolically given to the bride's parents, was turned over to the couple, and finally, by the time of the Middle Ages, our present-day custom arose of having the bride's family provide the dowry.

During the era of the Crusades, the life of the Jew was in constant jeopardy; bands of Crusaders could come through the town at any time and murder and rob the Jews. Parents of girls who had money for a dowry wished to have their daughters married at an early age, while they still had possession of the money, for if they were robbed, their daughter might have to remain unmarried for lack of a dowry. Parents of boys, on the other hand, wanted their sons married at an early age since married men were often excused from military service.

From the time of the Middle Ages, the *shadchan* (marriage broker) came into being. The word *shadchan* literally means "appeaser"— i.e., the man who appeased both the bride's and the groom's family, and settled all arrangements for the marriage. At first, he may have been a traveling salesman, traveling from town to town, arranging *shidduchim* (matches) between a girl in one town and a boy in another. Gradually *shadchanus* (arranging marriages) became a separate profession. The *shadchan* investigated the young man and woman whom he recommended for marriage, and had a set fee for his services. The *shadchan* had many things to consider in arranging these marriages: the socio-economic standing of the family, the type of young man, his interests and personality. On the bride's side, he had to consider the appearance of the bride, and whether she could cook. Once he felt that he had located a proper match, he had to arrange the negotiations for the dowry as well as the actual marital agreement. The business of a *shadchan* was a serious profession as well as a necessary one.

MARRIAGES IN BYGONE DAYS

Until late in the Middle Ages, there were three ceremonies connected with the wedding:

T'NAIM As soon as the *shadchan* had arranged the match, the parents of the bride and groom negotiated the terms of the dowry and other terms of the marriage. All of this was set forth in a contract called in Hebrew *T'naim* which literally means "stipulations." Often a fine or a penalty was imposed if either party wished to break the *shidduch* (match). The "bargain" was sealed with the breaking of a dinner plate symbolizing the fact that marital happiness can be shattered as easily as this broken dinner plate.

ERUSIN   The *Erusin* ceremony was the formal engagement of the couple. It differed from the modern concept of engagement in that a formal bill of divorce or *get* was necessary if the engagement was broken. At the *Erusin* ceremony the *Kesubah* or marriage contract was made, and the groom consecrated his bride. Through this consecration (*Kiddushin*), he prohibited her from marrying anyone else. The groom then presented a coin to his bride, acceptance of which symbolized her formal acceptance of her husband. The date for the *Nesuin,* or actual marriage ceremony, was then set.

NESUIN   The *Nesuin* was the formal marriage ceremony. From this time forth, the couple lived together. *Nesuin* comes from the Hebrew word meaning "carry." The bride was carried or escorted to the home of the groom.

Gradually, due to the uncertainty and fears of the Middle Ages, the *Erusin* and *Nesuin* ceremonies were held on the same day, the *Erusin* in the morning and the *Nesuin* in the afternoon. The Jewish wedding ceremony of today combines in one service the old formal engagement, which is immediately followed by the *Nesuin*—the wedding service. The coin, which was the symbol of the binding of the marriage, was changed to a ring.

THE WINE

Wine is traditionally used to sanctify all joyous Jewish ceremonies. The Talmud says that no religious ceremonies should be celebrated with beverages other than wine (Berachos 35a). In fact, the benediction recited over all fruit is that for the "fruit of the tree," but over wine a special benediction for the "fruit of the vine" is pronounced. It is no wonder, for the Bible has many noteworthy references to wine. The vine is used as a symbol of the qualities of goodness, peace and righteousness.

The bride and the groom sip wine, not once but twice: once for the *Erusin* and once for the *Nesuin,* the two combined parts of the modern marriage service. Sharing the same cup symbolizes in a beautiful manner the fact that they will share together all the pleasures and joys, problems and sorrows that their future life has in store for them. One is cautioned either to use two separate cups of wine, one for the *Erusin* and one for the *Nesuin,* or add a few drops of wine to the first cup, symbolically indicating that it is a separate and distinct cup. This is done in conformity with the precept expressed in the *Talmud* that one does not pronounce a blessing twice over the same cup of wine since this is considered as if one were taking the Lord's name in vain.

THE RABBI

A marriage is a contractual arrangement between two parties. According to Jewish law, therefore, no Rabbi is needed to solemnize a marriage ceremony. In fact, weddings used to take place in the bride's home, and the first record of a Rabbi officiating was in the fifteenth-century. The Rabbi of today performs a two-fold function at the marriage service: as an expert in Jewish law, he properly arranges the religious details, and as authorized by the state in which he resides, he performs the ceremony to meet the requirements of civil law. The marriage of the couple standing under the *chupah* (marriage canopy) is in accordance with both Jewish and civil law.

VEIL—*BEDEKEN* THE *KALLAH*

Brides of all faiths wear veils as they walk down the aisle for the marriage service, although few people know why. The veil originated in the time of Abraham. Abraham sent his servant Eliezer to Aram Naharaim to select a wife for his son, Isaac. The maiden Rebekah consented to return with Eliezer to Canaan. As they approached Abraham's tents where she was to meet her groom for the first time, Rebekah lowered her veil. From this time forth, the veil has been a symbol of modesty for the bride.

Today, a beautiful ceremony, often overlooked, is the ritual of covering the face of the bride with the veil immediately before the wedding ceremony. The drawing of the veil should be done by the groom, symbolically declaring that just as the veil now encircles the bride's face, so may his loving care encompass her from this time forth. It is a solemn moment when the groom turns to his bride and lowers her veil while those present witnessing the ceremony say:

"Our sister, be thou the mother of thousands of ten thousands."
(Genesis 24:60)

"May the Lord make you as Sarah, Rebekah, Rachel and Leah."

WEARING WHITE AND FASTING

According to Jewish tradition, the newlyweds begin a new life on their wedding day. The bride and groom do penance, and ask for forgiveness for their past sins in a manner very similar to the tradition of the High Holy Days. The bride and groom traditionally fast prior to their wedding service. The bride wears white, the color of purity, innocence and penance. In view of the new life they are about to enter, it is the custom for the bride and groom to wear new clothes on their wedding day.

Another custom that is seldom practiced today, was for the groom to wear a white *kittel* (robe) at the ceremony. Some have interpreted this as a sign of penance since the white *kittel* is also worn on the High Holy Days. Another interpretation of the wearing of the *kittel* is that it is a reminder of a shroud, worn so that the groom would realize that he must make his life worthwhile. A variant thought was that the *kittel* was a Jewish festive garment and therefore worn on one's wedding day. Of all the explanations, the last one seems most appropriate.

THE BRIDE AND GROOM UNDER THE CHUPAH

Jewish law and tradition seek to fulfill all the precepts of the Bible. In Psalms 45, which is a royal epithalamion, the following sentence appears:

"At thy right hand doth stand the queen in gold of Ophir."
(Psalms 45:10)

The Rabbis have interpreted this sentence to mean that the bride stands at the groom's right hand as they both face the Rabbi under the *chupah*. This is the reason for our custom today.

THE WEDDING RING

In days of yore, a coin would be given to the bride, the acceptance of which acknowledged the bride's agreement to the marriage. Today we use a ring instead of the coin to "seal the marriage," but note that the ring is placed on the forefinger of the bride's right hand so that the witnesses may see this act more clearly. For it is the act of handing over the ring and the recitation of the words:

"Harai at mekudeshes lee b'taba-as zoh k'das Moshe v'Yisrael
Behold, thou art consecrated unto me with this ring in accordance with the law of Moses and Israel."

by the groom that are the act of *Kiddushin* (consecration) itself. From this moment on, the bride is consecrated to her husband.

Jewish tradition prescribes that the ring should be a solid gold ring of definite value. The bride receiving the ring and beginning her married life, should enter the marriage without any possibility of deception. If the bride was presented with a jeweled ring, she might be accepting it on the basis that the jewels were genuine. Later on, finding out that the jewels were not real, she might contest the marriage, claiming fraud. The Rabbis wanted to avoid this, and since the twelfth-century ordained that a plain ring was to be used; however, it was ruled that if a ring with diamonds or other gems were, somehow, used, the marriage would nevertheless be valid.

CHUPAH

The *chupah* today is the canopy under which the marriage service takes place. The word *chupah* means "covered with garlands." Alternately, the entire ceremony is termed the *chupah,* because it takes place under the canopy.

Originally the *chupah* was the actual bridal chamber in which the bride awaited her groom for the marital union. Gradually, the actual chamber for the marriage passed into disuse and the symbolic canopy as we know it today came into being. In the days when the formal engagement and wedding were distinct ceremonies held on different days, the *chupah* was part of the actual *Nesuin* (wedding) ceremony only. When the bride and groom come under the *chupah* together, the bride officially leaves her father's domain and comes under the care of her husband.

THE BREAKING OF THE GLASS

In the year 586 B.C.E., the Babylonians conquered Palestine, devastated the land and destroyed the Temple. The Jewish people were carried into exile into the land of Babylonia. There they felt that they shouldn't "sing the song of the Lord in a foreign land," and pledged that they would never forget Jerusalem. According to the words of Psalm 137:

> "If I forget thee, O Jerusalem,
>   Let my right hand forget her cunning.
>   Let my tongue cleave to the roof of my mouth,
>   If I remember thee not;
>   If I set not Jerusalem
>   Above my chiefest joy."

Throughout Jewish history, one of the major thoughts which has held the Jewish people together has been their longing for the re-establishment of the Jewish state.

The Rabbis have said that one's "chiefest joy" was one's wedding day. Carrying out this pledge of the Jew, the groom recalls the destruction of the Temple through the simple act of breaking a glass on his wedding day. This has been the traditional explanation for the breaking of the glass at the conclusion of the marriage service.

The origin of this ceremony is not really known. The *Talmud* expresses surprise at the behavior of Rav Huna, who broke a glass at his own wedding. Surely if this rite were commonly practiced in those days, astonishment would not have been expressed. Therefore it seems to be a custom that started in the early centuries of the Common Era.

Some say that the origin of this rite was superstitious —a device to ward off the evil spirits. The breaking of the glass at the wedding may be compared to the breaking of a bottle on the bow of a new ship as it is being launched; the reason—to make noise, thereby warding off the evil spirits.

It is not important to find the origin of the custom, but rather to understand the meaning of the rite for our own day. The breaking of the glass has become as intrinsic a part of our marriage service as the wedding ring, or as the white bridal gown. The smashing of the glass is important because it symbolizes a connection of the couple with the Jewish people, its history and its traditions. The glass may also remind us how fragile a marriage really is; therefore it must be carefully regarded.

WEDDING TRADITIONS

1. It has been customary that two relatives (other than brothers and sisters) not be married on the same day. The reason for this has been that there are so very few occasions in life on which one can really celebrate, that two joyous celebrations should not take place on the same day. An exception to this rule is the marriage of brothers or sisters. They may be married on the same day, lest the expense of providing two separate wedding parties be too great for the family to bear.

2. *Aufruf*—literally, "to call up." On the Sabbath prior to the wedding day, the groom is called up to the Torah to honor his forthcoming marriage. Today, a special blessing is recited in honor of the bride and groom wishing them a happily married life. A custom, no longer practiced, was to take an extra Torah from the ark and to read a special portion relating to the marital arrangements between Isaac and Rebekah when the groom was called up to the Torah.

The wedding used to be a private family affair without a *minyan* (quorum of ten males) being present; only the two witnesses who signed the *Kesubah* (marriage contract) were needed. The communal phase of the wedding took place when the groom was called to the Torah on the

Sabbath prior to his marriage. The observance of the *auf-ruf* is still practiced today.

3. Ushers (*Unterfehrer-Shoshbienim*)—The function of the ushers at today's marriage services are completely honorary, although they had distinct responsibilities in bygone days. It was the function of the ushers to escort the bride and her family from their home to the synagogue. The ushers were needed since very often the people in the streets would gather around the bride and deter her. In addition, the bride's head was covered by a veil which prevented her from seeing where she was going.

THE *KESUBAH*

Jews were the first people to provide financial security for the woman. It was the man's obligation upon marriage to give to his wife a specific amount of money to be held by her and used in case of his death or in case the couple were divorced. Later on, this sum of money was given by the husband to the father of the bride, who held the money as a trustee for his daughter. Evidence is extant indicating that where the husband could not afford to place the money in escrow, items of furniture within the household were specifically designated as the property of the wife, so that she would be protected in case of her husband's death.

In year 80 before the Common Era, Rabbi Simon ben Shetach set up the *Kesubah* which was a marriage contract in which the husband agrees to undertake the obligation to have the stipulated amount of money set aside if he predeceases his wife or if he chooses to divorce her. This plan superseded the concept of actually setting aside the money. The *Kesubah* contains the provision granting 200 *zuzim* as a minimum payment to the bride if this was her first marriage, and 100 *zuzim* if a second or subsequent marriage. Today the value of a zuz is about fifteen cents, and thus is of symbolic significance only, but in ancient times this was equivalent to an insurance policy.

Today, too, part of the marriage service is the presentation to the bride of the *Kesubah* or marriage contract by the groom. It is a religiously binding document attested by two witnesses who declare that they observed the ceremony and saw the bride accept the ring, thereby consenting to the marriage. The agreement by the bride is necessary for a valid marriage. Her husband agrees to honor and support his wife, providing her with adequate clothing, food and shelter. Note that although the text of the *Kesubah* is hundreds of years old, it accords honor to the woman, for this is an attitude that is characteristic of the Jew. The contract becomes the property of the woman and is held by her as evidence of the marriage.

THE MARRIAGE SERVICE

The bride and the groom enter and stand under the *chupah*—the service then begins.

Blessed may you be who come in the name of the Lord.
We bless you out of the house of the Lord.
May He Who is mighty, blessed and great above all, send His
abounding blessings to the bridegroom and the bride.

"Blessed may you be . . ." a paraphrase from Psalm
118:26 welcoming the bridal party to the *chupah*. The
phrase *"Beruchim Habaim"* (blessed may you be) is frequently used as a greeting.

The blessings of *Erusin* (Engagement Service):

Blessed art Thou, O Lord our God, King of the universe, who
createst the fruit of the vine.

Blessed art Thou, O Lord our God, King of the universe, who
has hallowed us by Thy commandments, and has given us
command concerning the forbidden marriages; who has disallowed to us those who are betrothed, but has sanctified to us
those who are wedded to us by the *chupah* ceremony and the
covenant of wedlock.

Blessed art Thou, O Lord our God, who hallows Thy people
Israel with the *chupah* ceremony and the covenant of sacred
wedlock.

"Fruit of the vine"—blessing over the wine. The wine is
used to sanctify all joyous religious ceremonies. In the
two blessings of the *Erusin* (engagement) ceremony, we
read how God has sanctified the Jewish people by com-
manding whom they may and whom they may not marry.
Chapter eighteen of the Book of Leviticus contains the
list of close relatives one is not permitted to marry.

"Disallowed to us those who are betrothed . . ."—The Jewish state of engagement sets aside the bride from all men, even to the groom, until the marriage ceremony. In days of yore, often a year elapsed between the engagement (*Erusin*) and the marriage ceremony.

"Covenant of wedlock . . ."—Even in the days of the *shadchan* (marriage broker), Jews never considered a marriage a transaction but rather a sacred ceremony.

The groom places the ring on the right forefinger of his bride and says:

"Behold, thou art consecrated unto me by this ring, according to the law of Moses and of Israel."

"Behold thou art consecrated unto me . . ."—This is the declaration made by the groom to his bride. This declaration in addition to the acceptance by the bride constitutes the actual consecration of the marriage. The *Kesubah* is then read.

NESUIN (WEDDING CEREMONY)

The following are the seven blessings of the wedding ceremony, known in Hebrew as the *Sheva Berachos.*

1. Blessed art Thou, O Lord, our God, King of the universe, who creates the fruit of the vine.
2. Blessed art Thou, O Lord our God, King of the universe, who has created all things to his glory.

3. Blessed art Thou, O Lord our God, King of the universe, creator of man.

4. Blessed art Thou, O Lord our God, King of the universe, who has made man in His image, after His likeness, and has prepared unto him, out of His very self, a perpetual fabric of life. Blessed art Thou, O Lord, creator of man.

5. May she who is barren be exceedingly glad and exult, when her children are gathered within her in joy, Blessed art Thou, O Lord, who makes Zion joyful through her children.

6. O make these loved companions greatly to rejoice, even as of old, You did gladden Your creatures in the garden of Eden. Blessed art Thou, O Lord, who makes the bridegroom and the bride to rejoice.

7. Blessed art Thou, O Lord our God, King of the universe, who has created joy and gladness, the bridegroom and the bride, mirth and exaltation, pleasure and delight, love and brotherhood, peace and fellowship. Soon may there be heard in the cities of Judah and in the streets of Jerusalem, the voice of joy and gladness, the voice of the bridegroom and the voice of the bride, the jubilant voice of the bridegrooms from their marriage canopies, and the youths from their feasts of song. Blessed art Thou, O Lord, who makes the bridegroom to rejoice with the bride.

The seven blessings known as the "*Sheva Berachos*," constitute the marriage or *Nesuin* service today. The number of blessings to be pronounced at the wedding was not set till after Talmudic times, for the *Talmud* records a discussion of whether the number of blessings should be five, six or seven. The number seven was selected because of its association with good fortune. There are seven days of the week, *Rosh HaShanah* (New Year) occurs at the beginning of the seventh Hebrew month, *Shavuos* occurs seven weeks after Passover; the land, according to the Bible, is to lie fallow every seventh year, and after every seven sets of seven years is the fiftieth year of Jubilee.

The first of the seven blessings is over the wine. This is the second cup of wine that is sipped under the *chupah*. The first one is for the *Erusin* ceremony, and here it is for the *Nesuin* ceremony.

The second, third and fourth blessings are concerned with the idea that marriage is primarily for propagation. Surely, mankind cannot continue to exist without legitimate marriage. These blessings express the idea that God is the Creator of the universe, of man and of the institution of marriage.

The fifth blessing expresses the wish that the joy the bride and bridegroom feel on the day of their marriage may be shared by all the house of Israel, when Zion is restored.

The sixth blessing expresses the wish that this bride and groom may have the same happiness as did the first man, Adam and his wife, Eve.

The last blessing associates the happiness of the bride and groom with the Jewish people, with the hope of peace and brotherhood for them and for all the people of Israel in the near future.

The couple are then blessed by the Rabbi, the glass is broken and those assembled wish the bride and groom *"Mazel Tov!"* (Good Luck).

CHAPTER SIX

MOURNING

LEAVE TAKING

Funeral and mourning customs of all religions have the two-fold purpose of expressing honor and respect for the deceased, as well as providing comfort to the mourner. The Jewish approach to death and mourning shows keen insight and understanding of human needs at these times. Psychologists have often pointed out that Jews show proper respect for their deceased, and through the ritual, help the mourner adjust to his loss. While providing the mourner with the hope of immortality of his beloved, the keynote of the Jewish funeral is simplicity. The ritual comforts the mourners and gives them a better understanding of their own lives, and in many instances a better faith in God.

VISITING THE SICK

It is a great *mitzvah* in Judaism to visit the sick, which is called in Hebrew *Bikkur Cholim.* Jews make every effort to visit one who is ill, except, of course, if such a visit would be detrimental to the patient's health, or if the disease is contagious. The *Talmud* reports that Rabbi Akiba has said, "Anyone who does not visit the sick is as though he has shed blood." Rav Dimi said, "Everyone who visits an ill person adds to his life, and one who doesn't, brings death closer."

The *Talmud* specifies that the room of the seriously ill is not the place for levity, but rather for words of comfort. The visitor should not be the bearer of bad tidings in view of the fact that this might bring about a poor state of mind, and make recovery more difficult. Even if a seriously ill person asks about the welfare of a relative who has just died, one should not disclose this fact, so as not to impair the morale of the patient, and thereby hasten his death. Those who are ill are to be encouraged to maintain fine spirits, for the will to live often makes the difference between life and death.

CRITICALLY ILL

Judaism is opposed to euthanasia, for life is the gift of the Lord and only the "Lord giveth and the Lord taketh away" (Job 1:21). In addition it is always hoped that miraculously a cure for the critically ill may be found. However, even in instances when a physician sees absolutely no hope for recovery, one may not put the sick to death. Furthermore, one may not hasten the coming of death by withholding aid in the form of medicine, medical assistance, or even food. On the other hand, a physician may try an experimental drug on one seriously ill, even though its efficacy is not yet proven, if he feels that there may be a slight chance of helping the patient, since the saving of a life is of utmost importance.

According to Jewish custom, names have some mystical powers through which the person himself may be reached by the angel of death. When one is critically ill, it is customary to change his name so that the angel of death will be confused and will not be able to reach him. At times, when the name is changed, the name *Chayim* meaning "life" is added. Another custom, seldom practiced in our day, is to "change" the parents of a critically ill child by arranging for another couple to "buy" the child. By this rite, it is believed that the decree of death may be averted, once again by confusing the angel of death.

The person about to die should recite the confession,

asking for forgiveness for one's sins and confirming one's faith in God, and conclude with the words of the prayer *Shema Yisrael* (Hear, O Israel). The confession may be recited for one critically ill when he is unable to do so. Those in the room at the last moments, should rise in respect for the individual. The closest relative or eldest son should close the eyes of the deceased.

CREMATION

In view of the fact that Jews believe in the ultimate resurrection of the dead and the reuniting of the soul with the body, they are opposed to cremation, for destruction of the body would prevent resurrection. Despite the fact that there is no rule in the Bible or in the *Talmud* opposing cremation, it was practiced by the Jews only in the rarest instances. Cremation is indicated in the Book of Leviticus (20:14), as punishment for certain cases of incest. The Book of Joshua (7:15) also records a case where the bodies were burned in the case of a serious crime. Both of these instances indicate that the bodies were cremated as an added punishment to deter others from committing similar crimes.

The positive command to bury the dead stems from the passage in the Book of Deuteronomy (21:23), which states that "thou shalt surely bury him." Maimonides states that this definitely precludes cremation and directs that there shall be a burial. The *Shulchan Aruch* (Yoreh

De'ah 362) states "burial in the earth is a definite command." Jews today are opposed to cremation and therefore bury their deceased.

AUTOPSY

It is contrary to Jewish law to permit an autopsy unless there is a definite need for performing it. It is believed that any mutilation of the body would prevent resurrection. Instances when an autopsy would be permitted are: if the individual died of a strange illness and the autopsy would advance the cause of science, or if the illness might be of a hereditary nature whereby other members of the family might have benefit from the autopsy. If the civil authorities demand an autopsy, it is not within the province of the family to deny it.

SUICIDE

Jewish law indicates that there is to be no mourning for a person who commits suicide, but words of comfort shall be given to his bereaved relatives. Jews are very reluctant, however, to declare any death a genuine suicide. Instead, if there is any doubt at all, the full mourning ritual is observed, as, for example, when one is uncertain if the death is a suicide or a homicide. Circumstances such as suicide by a man who was mentally ill, or who was in a fit of rage do not bar his family from observing the full mourning ritual.

ONAIN

A person who is a close relative of the deceased is termed an *onain* from the time of death till after the funeral. He is exempt from the performance of all *mitzvos,* such as prayer, putting on *tephillin* (phylacteries), etc., so as to permit him, in all haste, to schedule the funeral. Even if the *onain* wishes to perform the *mitzvos,* he is prevented from doing so, since performance of the *mitzvos* would be regarded as not showing proper honor to the deceased. An *onain* is not subject to the laws of mourning; he may leave his home and may wear shoes as he makes arrangements for the funeral. He should not eat meat or drink wine as these are considered viands used for a feast and, therefore, unseemly for the *onain.* On the Sabbath, the *onain* is responsible for the performance of all the *mitzvos* and may eat whatever he desires.

PREPARING FOR THE FUNERAL

Every community used to have a *Chevra Kadisha* (Holy Society) whose responsibility it was to care for the body and prepare it for the funeral. Today, in many localities, the funeral directors have taken over these arrangements, and are often aided by appropriate synagogue committees.

TAHARAH

Taharah, or ritually cleansing the body, is necessary in preparing the body for burial, so that the individual may enter the Lord's presence in purity. *Tachrichim* (shrouds) of white linen cloth are then placed on the body. Men are buried with a *Tallis* (prayer shawl), with one of the *Tzisis* (fringes) cut to symbolize that those who have died are not responsible to observe the *Mitzvos.*

SHROUDS

Before the year 70 of the Common Era, when the Romans destroyed the Temple, Jews were buried in the clothes that they wore during their lifetime. Later, special and elaborate clothes were made for the deceased. This practice caused a great hardship on the poor who were unable to undertake this expense for their loved ones. Rabban Gamaliel, in the year 125 of the Common Era, introduced the custom, now practiced, of using simple linen shrouds for the rich and the poor alike. In death, he declared, all men are equal before God.

COFFIN

The custom of using coffins for burial seems to date back to the days of Joseph (Genesis 50:26)—"And he was put into a coffin in Egypt." The *Midrash Rabbah,* however, cites the story of Adam and Eve who "hid themselves within the trees of the garden," as the indication that burial should be in wooden coffins (Genesis Rabbah 19:8). Maimonides (Yad Abel 4.4) states it as a rule that burial should be in wooden coffins.

In accordance with the Jewish concept of equality of the rich and the poor alike in death, simplicity is the keynote of the day. A simple wooden coffin is most appropriate both in fulfilling the requisites of the concept of equality, as well as in conforming with the passage "Thou art dust and unto dust shalt thou return" (Genesis 3:19). The Rabbis have derived yet another rule from this passage—namely, that the dead are always to be buried in the ground.

RESPECT DUE TO THE DECEASED

Contrary to the practice in many communities, honor to the deceased, according to Jewish tradition, dictates that viewing of the body or kissing of the deceased is highly improper and disrespectful. It is important to remember how the individual looked in life and not in death.

Prior to the funeral it is not proper to serve food or to partake of food in the same room with the deceased, out of respect for him.

It is proper to engage an individual to watch the body from the time of death till the funeral. The *shomer* (watchman) recites *Tehillim* (Psalms). Today, most funeral homes can make such arrangements upon request.

After mentioning the name of the deceased, it is customary to say the words *Ahlav HaShalom* for men, and *Aleha HaShalom* for women. These words mean "May he/she rest in peace." Alternately, the words *Zichrono* (*Zichrona*) *LeVeracha,* meaning "May his/(her) memory be for blessing," are used.

FUNERAL

If an infant of less that thirty days dies, there is no service at burial, no shrouds are used, nor are any of the mourning customs such as *Kaddish* or *Shiva* practiced.

A mourner, who is less than thirteen years of age if a boy, or twelve years of age if a girl, is not obligated to observe any mourning customs. Although a minor is not required to practice mourning rites, if he understands his loss and expresses a desire to attend the funeral or to observe *Shiva*, it would not be proper to prevent him from doing so.

It is not proper to delay the funeral except if time is needed for relatives to arrive from a distance, or if time is required to obtain the casket or the shrouds. This is based on the passage from the Book of Deuteronomy (21:22,3) which states: "And if a man have committed a sin worthy of death, and he be put to death, . . . his body shall not remain all night upon the tree, but thou shalt surely bury him the same day." The Rabbis explained that the dignity of a human being must be respected even if he be a criminal. The criminal's execution atones for his sins, and his body shall be buried at the earliest moment. If such reverent treatment be accorded to an individual who is executed, how much more should it be extended to everyone else! So important is an early burial that funerals are permitted on the second day of *Yom Tov* (the second and eighth day of Passover, the second day of Sukkos, Simchas Torah, the second day of Shavuos) or the second day of Rosh HaShanah. Funerals are not permitted on the Sabbath, Yom Kippur, the first day of Rosh HaShanah, or Shavuos, the first and seventh day of Passover, the first day of Sukkos or Shemini Atzeres.

KERIAH

The Hebrew word *keriah* means "rending." It is the tearing of the garment as a sign of mourning. It used to be the practice to make a tear in the garment at the neck immediately after learning of the death of a near relative. Originally, *Keriah* was to be observed not only for close relatives, but also for leaders and wise men as well. Today, the rending of the garment is reserved for close relatives only and is done immediately before the beginning of the funeral service. In most communities, it is now customary to make a tear in a black ribbon pinned to one's attire, rather than ripping the garment itself. For one's parents, the *Keriah* is made on the left side, while for all other relatives the rent is made on the right side. One observes the rite of *Keriah* for the following relatives: father, mother, wife, husband, son, daughter, brother or sister.

A minor child (a girl who is less than twelve years old, and a boy who is less than thirteen years old), although exempt from all rites of mourning, is counseled to observe *Keriah*. Beginning at the time the child begins school, at about the age of six, the rite of Keriah is performed for him.

All *mitzvos* in Judaism are preceded with an appropriate blessing. The only exception to this rule among the six hundred and thirteen religious ordinances is *Keriah* for which there is no blessing. As the *onain* is exempt from all *mitzvos*, there is no blessing for *Keriah*. The only blessing that the *onain* does recite is "Blessed art Thou, O Lord, our God, Ruler of the universe, who art the righteous Judge." This blessing, accepting the will of God, is recited out of respect for the deceased.

One performs *Keriah* while one is standing. The Rabbis have deduced this rule from the Book of Job (1:20): "And Job stood up and rent his garment." With faith in God, Jews accept all their sorrows with perseverance, "standing up."

FUNERAL SERVICE

A very simple service is prescribed by Jewish law as a symbol of resignation and acceptance of the judgment of God. Jews have no liturgical or prescribed service for funerals. The .officiating Rabbi selects appropriate Psalms giving comfort to the bereaved and glorifying the virtues of the deceased. The service is concluded with the *Ail Maleh* prayer, asking God to have compassion upon the soul of the deceased.

THE EULOGY

According to Jewish tradition, there should be a eulogy for everyone. It is felt that there is some good in everyone, and it is important to extol their praise at the funeral service. The Rabbis cautioned that the eulogy should not be extravagant nor should virtues be ascribed to the deceased that are not really his.

Words of grief and lament combined with words of praise for the deceased comprise the eulogy of today. The origin of the eulogy stems from the Torah, where Abraham speaks words of lament over the loss of his wife, Sarah (Genesis, Chapter 23). A beautiful lament appears in the Second Book of Samuel (1:17–27) where David mourns the death of Saul and Jonathan:

Thy beauty, O Israel, upon thy high places is slain!
How are the mighty fallen!

Saul and Jonathan, the lovely and the pleasant
In their lives, even in their death, they were not divided;
They were swifter than eagles,
They were stronger than lions.
Ye daughters of Israel, weep over Saul,
Who clothed you in scarlet, with other delights,
Who put ornaments of gold upon your apparel.
How are the mighty fallen in the midst of battle!

FUNERAL IN THE DAYS OF YORE

The funeral of old was quite a bit different from the funeral of today. In days of yore, it was customary to have trumpets at funerals and to engage professional mourners to cry and to wail. A description of these professional mourners is found in the Book of Jeremiah (9:16).

"Consider ye, and call for the mourning women, that they
    may come
And send for the wise women that they may come."

The Jewish funeral of today in no way resembles this Biblical account of a funeral.

COMMITTAL SERVICE

At the cemetery, it is customary for the close relatives to bear the coffin to the grave, stopping seven times along the way. The seven stops represent the seven times that the word "vanity" is mentioned in the Book of Ecclesiastes

(1:2) in connection with life. Today, in many instances, the officiating Rabbi oversees the proper committal of the coffin to the grave to save any additional anguish to the bereaved family.

After the coffin is lowered into the grave, a spade of dirt is shoveled onto the casket. It is customary not to use the shovel in the regular manner, but to use the back or the side of the shovel, a means of reminding us that it is a human being that is being interred. As the casket is lowered into the grave, it is proper to say:

> *Al m'komo (m'komah) yavoh b'shalom*
> "May he (she) rest in peace."

The prayer called *Tzidduk Hadin* is also recited. It is at the gravesite that the mourners recite the *Kaddish* for the first time. Thereafter, all except the mourners form two lines and permit the mourners to pass, and as they do, the following is recited:

"May the Lord comfort you among all the other mourners of Zion and Jerusalem."

When the mourners arrive home, it is customary for them to wash their hands prior to entering their home. The cemetery is considered ritually unclean and the washing of one's hands ritually cleanses oneself.

SEUDAS HAVRA-AH

It is customary for friends or neighbors to bring to the house of mourning the first meal after the funeral. It is noted that the mourners probably would not prepare the meal if they had to prepare it themselves. Jewish custom suggests that the first meal include hard-boiled eggs. Eggs symbolize new life and hope for the future, and indicate that life must go on.

SHIVA

The word *Shiva* means "seven" in Hebrew and these are the seven days of mourning that follow the funeral.

HOW IS *SHIVA* COUNTED?

The day of the funeral is counted as the first day, even though the mourners may observe *Shiva* for only a few minutes on that day. On Fridays, the mourners observe *Shiva* till about noon and then they are permitted to prepare for the Sabbath. On the Sabbath, there is no mourning. Despite the fact that the mourners observe *Shiva* for only a few hours on Friday and not at all on the Sabbath, both of these days are counted in the seven-day mourning period. On the seventh day, one would "sit *Shiva*" for only one hour, but it counts for one complete day. If a funeral would take place on a Tuesday, for example, the mourners would count Tuesday as the first day and the seventh day would be the following Monday when they would observe the mourning for one hour only. Various Jewish holidays do interrupt or cancel the *Shiva* period. A Rabbi would guide the mourners in this respect.

HOW DID *SHIVA* ORIGINATE?

The first mention of any mourning is in the Book of Genesis. When Jacob dies, his son Joseph mourns for him for seven days. Later this was set as the initial phase of mourning.

FOR WHOM DOES ONE OBSERVE *SHIVA*?

The *Shiva* period is observed upon the passing of one's mother, father, son, daughter, wife, husband, brother or sister.

SHIVA OBSERVANCE

One should observe the *Shiva* for seven days. However, if one's business would greatly suffer, one may return after three days. The Rabbis indicate, however, that the first three days are for weeping and work is definitely prohibited. One who does not observe *Shiva*, according to the Talmud, is considered a callous person.

THE HOME DURING *SHIVA*

The primary purpose of the *Shiva* period is to enable relatives and friends to comfort the mourner and permit them to "talk out" their grief. It is, therefore, not proper for the mourner to be serving meals and elaborate refreshment for the callers. The atmosphere ought to be one that is proper for a house of mourning, not for a house of feasting. Callers who come should not greet the mourners. The mourners wear slippers which are not made of leather, sit on low stools, and refrain from shaving. All of these are signs of mourning.

THE SEVEN-DAY CANDLE

The mourner, upon arriving home, should light a candle that burns for seven days. The candle represents the soul of the departed. Just as the candle sheds light, so the deceased brought light into the household. One lights the candle in the home where one is "sitting *Shiva*." If the relatives are observing the *Shiva* period in several homes, then it would be proper to light a candle in each of these homes.

COVERING MIRRORS

It is a Jewish custom to cover all mirrors in the house of mourning, although the origin of the custom is obscure. One possible reason is that the mirror is used by the individual for primping and as such is a sign of vanity. At the time that one is observing the *Shiva* period, one should not concern himself with how one looks and with the frills of life, but rather ponder the values of life itself. Another possible explanation is that one should not see himself and how he looks while mourning.

OTHER *SHIVA* CUSTOMS

The mourner should remain at home during the *Shiva* period. If, however, the mourners choose to observe the mourning period together in one home, this would be entirely permitted. Under these circumstances, it is entirely permissible to return to one's own home each night to sleep.

Marital relations are prohibited during the *Shiva* period.

It is proper to wear dark clothes during the mourning, although wearing black is not obligatory for Jews.

Except for the first meal after the funeral, one is permitted to cook and prepare food, but only for one's immediate family.

GREETING OF THE MOURNERS IN THE SYNAGOGUE

On the Sabbath eve during the *Shiva* week, the mourner does not enter the synagogue during the *Kabbolas Shabbos* service (Service welcoming the Sabbath).

Immediately after the prayer, *Lecho Dodi,* when the Sabbath has been officially welcomed, the mourner enters the synagogue, while the congregation says: "May the Lord comfort you among the other mourners of Zion and Jerusalem."

THE FIRST YEAR

An individual should not participate in or attend joyous events for thirty days (*sheloshim*) when mourning for all close relatives, and for twelve months when mourning for one's mother and father. The Mourner's *Kaddish* is recited for a period of eleven months after the death of a loved one. It is recited at the three services, *Shacharis* (morning), *Mincha* (afternoon), and *Maariv* (evening service). On the Sabbath or on a holiday, it is also recited at the additional service for that day (*Musaf*).

THE MOURNER'S *KADDISH*

The Mourner's *Kaddish* is the traditional prayer recited by mourners, as they stand while reciting the prayer at religious services. It is strange to note that the prayer itself has no reference to death, to the deceased, or to mourning. It is a majestic prayer in praise of God recited by the mourner in the midst of his sorrow, in which he proclaims the justice of God, even though he is not able to comprehend all of His ways. At time of bereavement, the individual's faith is challenged, and through this prayer, the mourner reaffirms his faith in God.

It is proper for the community to provide a *minyan* (quorum of ten men) in the home of the mourner during the *Shiva* period each morning and evening so that he may pray and also be given the opportunity to recite the Mourner's *Kaddish*. Where this is not possible, the mourner is permitted to leave his home (putting on his shoes) to join the *minyan* in the synagogue. Under these circumstances, the mourner should not lead the congregation in prayer, nor should he be called for an *aliyah* before the Torah.

According to Jewish tradition, the virtues of the deceased are weighed against their misdeeds for entrance to *Gan Eden*, the after-life for the deserving. The recital of the Mourner's *Kaddish* by the mourner adds to the good deeds of the deceased. If, conceivably, an individual was completely evil, it is believed that if the Mourner's *Kaddish* were recited for a full twelve months, the deceased would be permitted to enter *Gan Eden* due to the merits added to his credit. Of course, nobody would want to think that a departed relative had been completely evil, yet he would want to assure him a place in *Gan Eden*. Thus, the Mourner's *Kaddish* is recited for a period of eleven months.

Traditionally the *Kaddish* is recited by the sons of the departed. If there are no sons, the responsibility rests with the brothers; or, if there are no brothers, the responsibility devolves on the father. Beyond these relatives, it is the closest male relative who is responsible for the recitation of the *Kaddish*. At times, certain difficulties arise preventing the responsible male from reciting the *Kaddish,* and another is hired to recite the Mourner's *Kaddish* in his place. Certainly more respect is shown when the relative himself recites the Mourner's *Kaddish;* therefore, the hiring of individuals should be reserved to those times when there are no male relatives to recite the *Kaddish.* Even if the relative cannot recite the *Kaddish* three times daily, he should recite it as often as possible. When another person is hired to recite the *Kaddish,* he should be directly cognizant for whom he is saying the *Kaddish.*

Customarily, women have not recited the Mourner's *Kaddish,* although they are responsible for observing the other mourning customs. But women are not prohibited from reciting the *Kaddish* when they attend services. In fact, women who are mourners should attend services regularly, particularly on Friday evening and Saturday morning, and should rise during the recitation of the Mourner's *Kaddish.* In doing so they will be bringing blessing upon their dear departed, in addition to the salutary effect this practice will have in bringing them closer to their faith.

It is curious to note that the *Kaddish* is one of the very few prayers in Jewish liturgy that was not written in Hebrew, but rather in a sister language, Aramaic, which was the spoken language during the Talmudic period. The origin of the Mourner's *Kaddish* stems from the custom of having a study session in the house of mourning, which was always concluded with a *Kaddish*. Gradually, it was the mourner who recited the *Kaddish*. The use of the vernacular (Aramaic) was because, no doubt, not everyone knew Hebrew.

VISITING THE CEMETERY

There is no definite rule about visiting the cemetery, although it is advisable not to visit the cemetery till at least thirty days have elapsed from the time of death. Visiting prior to the elapse of the month will reawaken the intense grief felt at the time of the passing of the deceased.

When visiting the cemetery, one will notice that pebbles or small stones are placed on top of the tombstones. This is a Jewish custom of unknown origin wherein the visitor to the grave expresses honor to the deceased through this practice. The pebbles display the fact that the grave was visited.

YAHRZEIT

Yahrzeit is the anniversary of the death of the individual, calculated according to the Jewish calendar. It is an annual day of commemoration. If the burial took place more than two days after the death, then the first *Yahrzeit* is observed on the anniversary of the date of the funeral, while the subsequent ones are on the anniversary of the day of death.

A twenty-four-hour candle, commonly called a *Yahrzeit* candle, is lit in the home of each mourner observing this day. It is customary to recite the Mourner's *Kaddish* on the day of the *Yahrzeit* and to observe the day solemnly. This is the time to give reflection and meditation on the merits of the deceased as well as to donate to charity in their behalf. It is a *Mitzvah* for the man who observes *Yahrzeit* to spend part of the day studying the Torah, leading the congregation in prayer, and being called for an *aliyah* to the Torah.

UNVEILING

Approximately at the end of the first year, it is customary to hold services at the gravesite, as the tombstone is unveiled and dedicated in memory of the deceased. A year is permitted to elapse before the unveiling, since surely the deceased is always remembered by the mourner due to his recitation of the Mourner's *Kaddish* during the first year.

A suitable tombstone is selected by the relatives on which the name of the departed is inscribed, together with the dates of birth and death, and often the relationships of the deceased. Two Hebrew abbreviations are often included on the stone. They are:

Pey nun, an abbreviation meaning "here rests."
Tav nun tzade beis hey, an abbreviation which means: "May his/her soul be bound up in the bonds of everlasting life."

Prior to the ceremony, a cloth is placed over the stone, so that it may be formally unveiled and dedicated in memory of the deceased.

As in the burial service, there is no set service for the Unveiling. The Rabbi officiating selects appropriate Psalms reflecting the qualities of the individual, and offers comfort to the mourners. The ceremony concludes with the *Ail Maleh* prayer:

O merciful God, who dwellest on high and art full of compassion, grant perfect rest beneath the shelter of Thy divine presence among the holy and pure who shine as the brightness of the firmament, to our departed   (name inserted here) who has gone to his eternal home. May his soul be bound up in the bond of eternal life. May the Lord be his heritage, and may he repose in peace. Amen.

THE CEMETERY

The terms for a cemetery in Hebrew all begin with the word *Bayis,* which means home, rather than the more obvious word *Sadeh,* which means "field." This is due to the fact that the grave is considered one's eternal home. The three terms for cemetery translated from the Hebrew are: house of graves, home of eternity and house of life (eternal life).

It is highly improper, and indeed it is a desecration of the cemetery, to bring food and drink there and to partake of food on cemetery grounds. This custom, though improper, seems to be widely practiced, but certainly should be discouraged. It is also important to be cautious on the cemetery grounds lest one step on a grave.

Out of respect for their deceased, it is the responsibility of every community to maintain a Jewish cemetery. It is possible for this cemetery to be adjacent to a non-Jewish one, provided there is a suitable fence or high shrubs separating the two cemeteries. At the time of the purchase of land for a cemetery, it should be duly consecrated.

YIZKOR

Yizkor is the prayer memorializing the dead that is recited in the synagogue four times a year, on Yom Kippur, Shemini Atzeres, the eighth day of Passover, and the second day of Shavuos. The word *Yizkor* means "May He Remember." Jews ask God to remember their deceased. *Yizkor* is not recited during the first year after death, since the individual is being remembered by the daily recitation of the Mourner's *Kaddish*.

EPILOGUE

And so we have covered the span of life, from birth to death, through the study of the rituals and attitudes of the Jew towards the milestones in his life. It is hoped that a better understanding of these events of life has been realized which will lead to a more meaningful observance of the rituals. For Judaism reflects a keen relationship between man and his Maker contributing to a fond appreciation of life.

Although this book is not intended to be a complete and exhaustive study of all the details and laws, for such a study would fill many a volume, I trust that this volume has provided a basic foundation and background that will lead to further study of the imperishable and inspiring heritage of the Jewish people.

GLOSSARY

Ail Maleh—Prayer for the deceased asking God's compassion for them. Prayer is recited at funerals, unveilings and at *Yizkor*.

Aliyah (Plural: *aliyos*)—The honor of being called to the Torah at the time it is being read in the synagogue.

Ashkenazim—Jews who follow the tradition that grew up in north and central Europe.

Aufruf—The groom is called up to the Torah on the Sabbath prior to his wedding day.

Ba'al—The husband.

Bar Mitzvah (for girls: *Bas Mitzvah*)—One who is responsible for observing the *mitzvos* (religious ordinances); also the ceremony upon assumption of this responsibility.

Bar Onshin—One who is legally liable for any deeds of misconduct.

Bikkur Cholim—Visiting the sick.

Bris—The covenant; the circumcision.

Chayim—Life.

Chevra Kadisha—Literally "holy society"; the group that is responsible to prepare a body for burial.

Chol HaMoed—The intermediate days of Passover and Sukkos.

Chupah—The wedding canopy under which the service is held.

Derashah—Sermon.

Erusin—Betrothal.

Gaonim—Heads of the academies in Sura and Pumbedita; judicial authority.

Gemorah—Commentary and supplement to the *Mishnah.* Part of the Talmud.

Haftorah—Portion of the prophets that is assigned for reading during the synagogue service.

Halitzah—Ceremony in which man declares he does not wish to enter Levirate marriage and frees the woman to marry whom she wishes.

Kabbolas Shabbos—Service welcoming the Sabbath.

Kaddish—A doxology recited during religious services. The Mourner's Kaddish is the doxology recited by the mourners.

Keriah—Rending of the garment as a sign of mourning.

Kesubah—The Jewish marriage contract.

Kiddush—"Sanctification" Prayer proclaiming the sanctity of a holy day or the Sabbath.

Kohen—Descendant from the priestly family.

Kvater, Kvaterin—Godfather, godmother—appointed at the time of the Bris.

Maariv—The evening service.

Minchah—The afternoon service.

Minyan—The quorum of ten males needed for a service.

Mishnah—Collection of the oral law . . . part of the Talmud.

Mitzvah (Plural: *mitzvos*)—A religious ordinance.

Mohel—A religiously approved person who performs the circumcision.

Musaf—The additional service recited on the Sabbath and Jewish holidays.

Nesuin—Marriage.

Onain—The mourner prior to the funeral.

Os HaBris—The sign of the covenant.

Passover—Jewish holiday commemorating the exodus of the Israelites from Egypt.

Pidyon HaBen—Redemption of the first-born.

P'ru u'r'vu—Be fruitful and multiply.

Rosh Chodesh—The beginning of a new month.

Rosh HaShanah—Jewish New Year.

Sandek—The individual honored with the duty of holding the child during the *Bris*.

Sephardim—The Jews who practice the tradition which grew up on the Iberian peninsula.

Seudah—Feast.

Seudas Havra-ah—The meal offered to the mourners upon their return from the cemetery.

Seudah Shel Mitzvah—A festive meal in connection with a joyous milestone in life.

Shacharis—The morning service.

Shadchan—Marriage broker.

Shalom Zachor—Ceremony welcoming the new lad.

Shavuos—The Jewish holiday of Pentecost.

Sheloshim—The first thirty days of the mourning period.

Shemini Atzeres—Holiday: Eighth Day of Solemn Assembly.

Sheva Berachos—The seven wedding blessings.

Shidduch—Popular expression denoting a "match," marriage, or betrothal.

Shiva Asar B'Tammuz—17th day of the Hebrew month of Tammuz; a fast day in commemoration of the beginning of the downfall of the city of Jerusalem in 586 B.C.E.

Shulchan Aruch—Code of Jewish law written by Joseph Karo.

Simchas Torah—A Jewish holiday celebrating the completion of the reading cycle of the Torah.

Shiva—Seven; the seven days of mourning.

Sukkos—Feast of Tabernacles.

Tachrichim—Shrouds.

Taharah—Ritual cleansing of the body prior to the funeral.

Takkanah—Ordinance, innovation.

Talmud—Compendium of Jewish Law.

Tehillim—Book of Psalms.

Tephillin—Phylacteries.

T'naim—Stipulations concerning a proposed marriage.

Tisha B'Av—Ninth day of the month of Av; commemorates the destruction of the first and the second Temples that stood in Jerusalem.

Torah—The five books of Moses; namely, Genesis, Exodus, Leviticus, Numbers, Deuteronomy.

Tzedekah—Literally "Righteousness"; charity.

Tzidduk HaDin—Prayer recited at funerals.

Tzisis—Fringes of the Tallis (prayer shawl).

Yahrzeit—Anniversary of the death of an individual.

Yitzchak—Isaac.

Yizkor—Memorial prayer.

Yom Kippur—Day of Atonement.
Yom Tov—Jewish holiday.
Zohar—Mystical commentary on the Bible.
Zuz, Zuzim—Coins in use in Talmudic days.

INDEX